PROCLAIMING
CHRISTMAS

PROCLAIMING CHRISTMAS

PROCLAIMING
CHRISTMAS

40 timeless talks and sermons

Edited by **J.John**

Published in the UK by Philo Trust

Copyright © 2012 J.John

Published 2012 by Philo Trust, Witton House, Lower Road, Chorleywood,
Rickmansworth, WD3 5LB, United Kingdom

www.philotrust.com

The right of J.John to be identified as the Editor of this Work has been asserted
by him in accordance with the Copyright, Designs and Patents Act 1988.

British Library Cataloguing in Publication Data

A catalogue record for this book is available from the British Library

ISBN-978-0-9573890-0-7

Cover design by Chris Jones

Page layout by Verité CM

Printed and bound in the UK

CONTENTS

PREFACE – *J. John*

1   **LIFE: IT'S YOURS TO CHOOSE** – *Simon Allaby*

2   **THE INVITATION** – *Stuart Bell*

3   **THE SHEPHERDS (LUKE 2:8–20)** – *John Benson*

4   **JOY, PEACE AND THE MEANING OF CHRISTMAS** – *Joe Boot*

5   **WHAT WILL YOU BE WEARING THIS CHRISTMAS?** – *David Brickner*

6   **FINGERPRINTS OF GOD** – *Erin Clifford*

7   **THE GOD WHO WORKS FROM BACK TO FRONT** – *Bayless Conley*

8   **NAME ABOVE ALL NAMES** – *Gavin Collins*

9   **CHRISTMAS IN A NUTSHELL!** – *Jodie Collins*

10   **WHAT WOULD JESUS SAY TO SANTA CLAUS?** – *Mark Conner*

11   **INDESCRIBABLE!** – *Anthony Delaney*

12   **THE QUEEN'S SPEECH** – *Greg Downes*

13   **REFOCUSING THE LENS OF CHRISTMAS** – *Alison Fenning*

14   **THE PROBLEM WITH CHRISTMAS!** – *Mark Greenwood*

15   **SHOULD CHRISTMAS BE BANNED?** – *Greg Haslam*

16   **FOUNDATION FOR THE STUDY OF INFANT DEATHS CAROL SERVICE** – *Graham James*

17   **THE GIFT** – *J. John*

18   **MORE THAN A CHRISTMAS CAROL** – *J. John*

19   **THE FIRST GREAT AWAKENING** – *R. T. Kendall*

20   **PREFER ONE ANOTHER: SELFLESSNESS** – *David McDougall*

21 **EMMANUEL: GOD IS WITH US** – *Simon McIntyre*

22 **MERRY CHRISTMAS, EVERYONE!** – *Keith 'Mitch' Mitchell*

23 **THE BIRTH OF JESUS** – *Nigel Mumford*

24 **WHAT IF THERE WAS NO CHRISTMAS?** – *Rich Nathan*

25 **MEET THE REAL JESUS** – *Haydn Nelson*

26 **THE GIFT OF CHRISTMAS UNWRAPPED** – *Ed Olsworth-Peter*

27 **CHRISTMAS EVE** – *Paul Perkin*

28 **PEACE *(SHALOM)* ON EARTH: THE MESSAGE OF THE SEASON!**
                                          – *Susan Perlman*

29 **CAN YOU FIND GOD?** – *John Peters*

30 **THE BEST CHRISTMAS PRESENT EVER** – *David C.L. Prior*

31 **FESTIVE RUBBISH** – *Mark Ritchie*

32 **YOU CAN'T ALWAYS GET WHAT YOU WANT; BUT YOU GET WHAT YOU NEED** – *Chris Russell*

33 **THE FOUR Cs OF CHRISTMAS** – *Mark Russell*

34 **STAND UP TO RECEIVE THE GIFT OF CHRISTMAS** – *Tim Saiet*

35 **THE TRUE CHRISTMAS STORY** – *David Shearman*

36 **GAFFA TAPE GOSPEL** – *Will Van Der Hart*

37 **GATHERED TO THE LIGHT** – *Justin Welby*

38 **THE WONDER OF CHRISTMAS PRESENCE** – *Paul Williams*

39 **THE GOVERNMENT WILL BE ON HIS SHOULDERS** – *N.T. Wright*

40 **CHRISTMAS SWORD** – *Philip Yancey*

PREFACE
J.John

Christmas comes out of an ancient past, yet there is always something refreshingly new about it. In the stable there lay all the hopes of thousands of years of recorded history. Christmas is the time and place where God pulls back the curtain so we can see his face. Christmas is the answer to our questions, 'Where is God?' 'Who is God?'

There was once a farmer who did not believe in the Christmas story. He thought the idea that God would become a man was absurd. His wife, however, was a Christian. The farmer gave her a hard time, mocking her faith. 'It's all nonsense; why would God lower himself to become a human like us? It's such a ridiculous story.'

One snowy Christmas Day, his wife went to church while the farmer stayed at home. After she had left, the weather deteriorated into a blinding snowstorm. Then he heard a loud thump against the window – then another thump.

He went outside to see what was happening. There in the field was a flock of geese! They had been migrating but had become disorientated by the storm and were stranded on his farm, unable to fly or see their way. The farmer wanted to help them and realised his barn would give them shelter for the night. He opened the barn door and stood back, hoping they would make their way in but they didn't realise it would be shelter for them. So he tried to shoo the geese in, but they ran in all directions. Perplexed, he got some bread and made a trail to the barn door. But they still didn't catch on – nothing he could do would get them into the warmth and shelter of the barn.

Feeling totally frustrated, he exclaimed, 'Why don't they follow me? Can't they see this is the only place where they can survive the storm? How can I possibly get them to follow me?' He thought for a moment and then realised that they would not follow a human. He said to himself, 'How can I possibly save them? The only way would be if I could become like one of them. Then I could save them. They would follow me and I would lead them to safety.'

At that moment he realised what he had said. The words reverberated in his head: 'If only I could become like one of them, then I could save them.' Then, he understood God's heart towards humankind. God couldn't have made himself bigger to impress us, so he made himself smaller to attract us.

On 29 July 1969, astronaut Neil Armstrong climbed down a ladder and put his feet on the surface of the moon. In an address, President Richard Nixon said, 'The greatest event in human history occurred when man first put his foot on the moon.' Astronaut Hale Irwin responded, 'The most significant achievement of our age is not that man stood on the moon, but rather that God in Christ stood on the earth.'

One of the most enjoyable things I do is read sermons! I have read the sermons of John Wesley, George Whitefield, Charles Finney, D.L. Moody, Smith Wigglesworth, Dietrich Bonhoeffer and many others. I believe the most fertile season of the year is Christmas and I have been privileged to have spoken at more than 500 Christmas carol services over the last thirty years. So I thought it would be good to have a collection of sermons that leaders, ministers and anyone else can dip into and find inspiration from the numerous perspectives. So I asked thirty-eight friends of mine to each send me one of their Christmas sermons and I am delighted to offer this collection and grateful to each contributor for offering their sermon. The collection includes two of my own and they are all arranged in alphabetical order by contributor. Some are like the 'starter' for a meal, others the 'main course' and others the 'dessert'. The contributors represent a number of denominations and church streams and range from writers to evangelists, from bishops to theologians. Each sermon has been abridged to approximately 1,000 words, but I hope that what you read reflects the essence of each original contribution.

In the words of John Wesley, may these sermons 'strangely warm our hearts' and inspire us in our own journey of faith. If you are a preacher, I pray that you will be enriched and inspired with new perspectives and ideas for your own preaching at Christmas.

I conclude with this inspiring Christmas Eve greeting from a letter written in 1513 by Giovanni da Fiesole to his friend, Countess Allagia Aldobrandeschi.

> *I salute you. I am your friend, and my love for you goes deep. There is nothing I can give you which you have not already; but there is much, very much, which though I cannot give it, you can take. No heaven can come to us unless our hearts find rest in today. Take heaven. No peace lies in the future which is not hidden in this precious little instant. Take peace. The gloom of the world is but a shadow. Behind it, yet within our reach, is joy. There is radiance and courage in the darkness could we but see it; and to see, we have only to look. Life is so generous a giver, but we, judging its gifts by their coverings, cast them away as ugly or heavy or hard. Remove the covering, and you will find beneath it a living splendour, woven of love, and wisdom, and power. Welcome it, greet it, and you touch the angel's hand that brings it.*

> *Everything we call a trial, a sorrow, a duty, believe me, that angel's hand is there, the gift is there, and the wonder of an overshadowing Presence. Our joys, too, be not content with them as joys. They, too, conceal diviner gifts. Life is so full of meaning and purpose, so full of beauty beneath its covering, that you will find earth but cloaks your heaven. Courage, then, to claim it, that is all! But courage you have, and the knowledge that we are pilgrims wending through unknown country our way home.*

> *And so, at this Christmas time, I greet you, not quite as the world sends greeting, but with profound esteem now and for ever.*

> *The day breaks and the shadows flee away.*

LIFE: IT'S YOURS TO CHOOSE
Simon Allaby

When I was a child my family and I spent Christmas with an aunt and uncle. They had a hearth in their lounge that they did not use, so at Christmas my aunt decorated it by laying a bed of newspaper in the grate, and filling it with pinecones sprayed with gold and silver paint – highly inflammable paint, as it was to turn out!

One afternoon, when I was about 8 years old, I was alone in the lounge with nothing to do. As I looked around the room I spotted my uncle's silver lighter on the mantelpiece. I took it and lit the corner of the newspaper on which the pinecones were resting. I let it burn for a few seconds and then quickly blew it out. I tried again and this time let the paper burn a bit longer before blowing out the flames. Emboldened by my newfound skill as the 'King of Flames', I lit the paper a third time and let it burn even longer than before. However, by the time I attempted to blow the flames out this time, they had caught hold and my frantic efforts served instead to encourage them. Very quickly my aunt's decorative pinecones had become a roaring inferno.

I returned the lighter to the mantelpiece and sat back on the sofa. After a few minutes my mum came in, registered surprise that the fire was now lit and asked who had lit it. Without a moment's hesitation I said that my uncle must have done so. My mum accepted this explanation but my sense of relief was short lived, as the next person to come in was my uncle, who also registered surprise and also asked who had lit the fire. At this point it became obvious to my mum that I had done so. Despite my vigorous denials I was in trouble – and seem to remember being sent to bed early that evening!

I learned two things that day that I have never forgotten: first, that I knew the difference between right and wrong and that I could freely choose to deliberately do something that I knew was wrong; and secondly, that if I did so I would spoil a relationship that was very precious to me – my relationship with my mum.

Well, the Bible says that we are all like that – as human beings we know the difference between right and wrong, and when we choose to do wrong we spoil relationships with the people we love, and most especially with the God who created us and who loves us with all of his heart. The apostle Paul put it like this: 'For all have sinned and fall short of the glory of God' (Romans 3:23). Paul is saying that God is perfect and we are not, and that means we are separated from the God who loves us, and unless something happens to change that state of affairs it will remain the case for eternity.

Many of us know that we have done wrong, and for many people this sense of guilt and shame keeps them from approaching God. I have often heard people say something along the lines of, 'Surely God wouldn't want anything to do with me, after all that I've done?' Such people see God as out to punish them for what they have done wrong – better then to keep at a safe distance! The reality, however, is that while God *is* a God of justice, he is also a God of love whose primary desire is to restore us.

God loves us so much that he is not prepared to leave us as we are – separated from him and without hope. In Jesus, God comes looking for us, to tell us how much he loves us and show us the way back to him. This baby, whose birth we are preparing to celebrate once again, grew up, went to a cross and died in our place, for all our sins and wrongdoing, so that the barrier of sin between us and our heavenly Father might be removed once and for all.

One of the most famous verses in the Bible is John 3:16 – 'For God so loved the world that he gave his one and only Son, that whoever believes in him shall not perish but have eternal life.' John wrote his Gospel having lived alongside Jesus for three years, and after a lifetime spent reflecting on who Jesus was and what he had come to do, and this verse sums up what he had concluded: Jesus came to show us the full extent of God's love for us, and on the cross make it possible for us to once again enter into relationship with him. But John is also clear that Jesus offers us a choice that we must take if we are to enjoy this relationship. We must believe in Jesus and receive him into our lives – if we do then we will enjoy eternal life, but if we don't then our relationship with our heavenly Father will remain broken.

So we find ourselves in a place where to do nothing, or to make the wrong choice, will cause us to remain separated from God's love. But because God loves us so much, Jesus came to show us that there is a choice that leads to life – fullness of life in this world and eternal life in the world to come. That's the Christmas story and that's the Good News we are preparing to celebrate. What choice will you make?

Revd Simon Allaby is the director of the 6:19 Trust (www.sixnineteen.co.uk). Launched in 2009, the Trust has the twin aims of seeing the Good News of Jesus proclaimed and equipping and encouraging the church to evangelise. Simon was ordained in 1990 and has served as a full-time church leader in a number of churches in Durham and Sussex. As part of his work with 6:19 Simon leads a church in Bolney, Sussex, where he lives with his wife and three children.

THE INVITATION
Stuart Bell

God's invitation list is often different from our own.

In Matthew 22 Jesus tells the story of a special banquet. Invitations were sent to many, but people refused to attend. A second opportunity was given and again people refused. Then, the master says, 'Go to the street corners and invite to the banquet anyone you find' (Matthew 22:9). Often the people we least expect respond first to the invitation.

On the first Christmas God invited the most unexpected people to be the first to see his Son. Shepherds were among the lowest in society but he invited them first. I want us to think about invitations.

An invitation outlines the importance of the event

I have conducted a lot of weddings through the years and I've seen some incredible designs for invitations. They have become ever more creative and colourful. Other cards are similarly inventive. We now have birthday cards that open up and play music. You can open a Christmas card and hear Bing Crosby personally sing 'White Christmas' just to you. However, the event has to match the invitation. When God invited the shepherds to see his Son it involved a personal invitation from the powerful archangel Gabriel followed by full technicolour, top-quality sounds produced by the mass choirs of the angel hosts. This was declared to be good news of great joy for all the people.

An invitation gives details of the venue and time of the event

Missing details off an invitation or getting the wrong date or time can cause confusion. God's invitation was pretty thorough. 'Today in the town of David [Bethlehem] a Saviour has been born to you; he is the Messiah, the Lord. This will be a sign to you: you will find a baby wrapped in cloths and lying in a manger' (Luke 2:11–12). I doubt whether any other babies born in Bethlehem were laid in animal feeding troughs. Later, when wise men respond to the invitation, God arranges a cosmic phenomenon known as his star to light up the place.

An invitation needs a response: RSVP

The shepherds' response was immediate. '"Let's go to Bethlehem and see this thing that has happened, which the Lord has told us about." So they hurried off and found Mary and Joseph, and the baby, who was lying in the manger' (Luke 2:15–16). In Jesus' story as related in Matthew's Gospel many refused the invitation to the banquet. We can refuse, saying that we're not ready, or we can say yes to the greatest adventure of our lives.

A Christmas prayer

Dear God, thank you for the invitation that you give people this Christmas time to know Jesus. Thank you that God sent his one and only Son to die on a cross that I may receive the gift of eternal life. I am sorry for my sins, please forgive me. I gladly accept your wonderful invitation. Please come into my life. I invite you to be my Saviour, friend and Lord. Amen.

Pastor Stuart Bell is the Senior Leader of New Life Lincoln (www.newlifelincoln.org.uk), a church of 1,000+ people. Stuart is also Leader of the Ground Level Network, a network of over 100 churches. He works with a growing group of international leaders known as Partners for Influence. The group is missional and is working across different streams and denominations, bringing Kingdom perspectives and values. Their desire is to see strong, effective, healthy churches partnering together for greater influence. Stuart is a speaker and teacher and has written four books. Married to Irene, he has three children and three grandsons.

THE SHEPHERDS (LUKE 2:8–20)
John Benson

Q: Does anyone know how many shepherds there were on the hills near Bethlehem?

Q: Does anyone know the names of the shepherds?

I have been trying to think what their names might have been and I am going to introduce them to you now. I will need seven helpers …

Shepherd 1 – SLEEPY

Some people are much heavier sleepers than others. They find it very hard to wake up. Sleepy was like that. He was asleep when the angel first appeared. His friends were so frightened that they woke him up. Sleepy was nearly awake when the angel spoke of a special baby being born.

Shepherd 2 – GRUMPY

Most families have someone like this – nothing is ever right for them. 'Why do we have to go to church before we can open all our presents?'

Grumpy was grumpy as usual: 'Who do those angels think they are, disturbing us in the middle of the night? Why should we go all the way to Bethlehem? Who will look after the sheep while we are away? We might lose our jobs if we lose any sheep.'

Shepherd 3 – SNEEZY

Sneezy should never have been a shepherd. Hay fever and working in the fields with grass and sheep didn't really go together well.

'Let's go to Bethlehem and see what has happened … (sneeze) … if nothing else I might stop sneezing for a while.'

Shepherd 4 – DOC

He was the wise one, the one who was used to taking charge. He had been just as frightened as the others when the angel spoke to them, but now he had pulled himself together.

'Come on! Let's get going to Bethlehem. Our sheep can look after themselves for one night. The angel said that the baby would be lying in a manger and I think I know where we will find him. Let's go and see.'

Shepherd 5 – BASHFUL

He was not the most forceful of the shepherds. He almost seemed to need permission from the sheep before he did anything.

'Do you think it's OK to go bursting in to this stable? The baby has only just been born. Shouldn't we let the mother rest? And he's supposed to be a very special baby – would it be right for us to go and see him?'

The others just left him outside and carried on in to see the baby in the manger.

Shepherd 6 – HAPPY

Happy went in. He saw the baby Jesus just as the angel had described. He saw the baby who is also the Saviour and Christ the Lord. Happy knew that this was joyful good news, just as the angel had said.

'God does care for his people. God has kept his promise to send us a Saviour. God is about to do great things for us … and we have the privilege of being in on it from the beginning.'

Only as we look beyond the baby of Bethlehem to the Lord and Saviour can we share in this joy. The baby of Bethlehem grew up:

- Jesus went around preaching the good news of the Kingdom of God.
- Jesus healed many sick people and even raised some dead people to life.

- Jesus taught that he came to give his life as a ransom for many.
- Jesus was arrested in his 30s and killed on a cross. He died praying, 'Father, forgive them!'

The baby of Bethlehem grew up into the suffering servant of Good Friday and the risen Lord of Easter Day. After convincing his friends that he really was alive again he ascended into heaven. He has promised that he will return again.

Take away the Saviour who is Christ the Lord and all that you have left is Xmas – an expensive mid-winter celebration to give short-term relief to busy lives.

Q: Can anyone guess the name of my last shepherd?

Shepherd 7 – DOPEY

Dopey never did understand what it was all about. He saw the angel. He listened to the message of the angel. He went with the other shepherds to Bethlehem and saw the new-born baby – but that is all that he saw. The others explained it all to him again and again but he still could not take it in.

Don't be 'dopey' by joining in Christmas celebrations without ever taking in why Jesus came.

Many seem to be content with a Christ-less thing they call Xmas. If that is where you are today I want to leave you with some questions about Jesus:

- What if it is true?
- What if there is a God?
- What if Jesus really did come from God?
- What if I do need a Saviour?
- What if I must eventually bow down to Jesus as my Lord?

If that is where you are, then this becomes the most important issue for this Christmas – more important than food, family and presents. Make some space to think about Jesus.

But for those of us who recognise Jesus as the Saviour who is Christ the Lord, Christmas becomes a time for joyful celebration as we believe and trust in him.

Endnote:

The props for this sermon were seven cardboard cut-out shepherds in bright colours. Each was about 1 metre high and attached to a thin pole for a child to hold up so that it could be seen by the whole congregation. These could be replaced by wrap-around shepherd costumes for seven volunteer children. The children can be encouraged to act up to the name they are given.

PowerPoint images could be used, but this would reduce the involvement of the congregation – and remove the exciting but unpredictable challenge of interacting with the children!

The congregation gradually realised the origin of the names of the shepherds. Some began to think how the other names that had not yet been used could be tied in to the passage – some even opened up a Bible to take a fresh look.

The Revd Canon Dr John Benson is a retired clergyman living in Chester. Before retirement he served in the Diocese of Singapore for twenty years. His roles there included Vicar of St George's Church, Director of Training for the Diocese, Dean of Cambodia, Dean of Laos and Vicar of the Chapel of the Resurrection. He is still actively involved in preaching and in mentoring clergy and church workers. John is married to Anita and they have two married daughters.

JOY, PEACE AND THE MEANING OF CHRISTMAS
Joe Boot

Christmas is meant to be a time of celebration and a time of joy – but why? And why is it that so few people seem to benefit from this message of joy in their own lives? How can we truly experience the joy of Christmas? These are the questions I want to seek to answer.

In Luke 2:10–11 we read the words of the angel to the shepherds: 'Do not be afraid. I bring you good news that will cause great joy for all the people. Today in the town of David a Saviour has been born to you; he is the Messiah, the Lord.' We live in an age equally in need of the joy of this good news. In fact, our historical moment is one in which joy is in short supply.

Joy involves gladness, satisfaction and rest. We all know that the birth of a baby is usually a time of great joy and excitement as that small miracle takes place when a precious new life comes into the world. But how can the birth of Jesus be good news for *all* people? As joyful as a birth can be, why and how is this birth more special than all the other births that take place every day? The famous Christmas carol puts it like this: 'Joy to the world, the Lord is come, let earth receive her king.' Notice the themes: the reason for joy is that the baby is a king, the Son of God, the Lord whose Kingdom and reign will never end. And it is *because* of the God-man Jesus Christ, born Saviour and King, that you and I have reason for real joy and gladness.

In order to experience the joy of this 'good news', we must first understand and rightly see ourselves and our nature. Psalm 8 tells us that men and women were created by God with great nobility (Psalm

8:5). But in popular thought today 'salvation' is seen as merely 'being (or *finding*) yourself'. This view of salvation results in being self-centred and living as your own god. But we are not God: we struggle with boredom, anxiety and inconstancy; we grow old, we get ill and we die! Instead of realising that our lack of joy results from believing the lie that we can live as our own god and saviour, we feel thwarted in our pursuit of joy and happiness. We then see ourselves as innocent victims of God and time, and end up hating both. But this lie cannot bring freedom and joy, or salvation; it just makes us slaves of sin and self. However, the salvation announced in Christ is deliverance, wholeness, victory and resurrection, and that *is* cause for joy. The starting point of discovering Christmas joy, then, is recognising that we are not primarily victims, but sinners and rebels in need of good news.

The second great gift at Christmas is peace. On that first Christmas, angels declared a message of peace: 'Glory to God in the highest heaven, and on earth peace to those on whom his favour rests' (Luke 2:14, TNIV). We live in a world that is much in need of the peace of God: in world affairs, in our communities, families, homes and, before anything else, in our own hearts. Everywhere, men and women seek peace of mind and heart, and find it elusive; many of us may feel anything but peace with God, with ourselves, or even with those closest to us at Christmas.

Scripture makes clear that Christ came to *preach* and *make peace*, with and for us. Paul writes, 'He came and preached peace to you who were far away and peace to those who were near' (Ephesians 2:17). Christ is called the 'Prince of Peace' (Isaiah 9:6), for his peace is a royal peace. The message of Christmas is that there is a peace available in and through Christ that 'passes knowledge'. Yet the question remains, how can a Jewish infant born to a peasant family in first-century Palestine (then a Roman province) be the source of peace with God and man for twenty-first-century Gentiles?

Peace, true peace, is a *by-product* of the work and ministry of Jesus Christ in history and in our lives personally. If we want peace from a troubled conscience due to sin, peace with God, peace in heart and mind, peace about the future, we cannot find it outside of Jesus Christ! He himself is our peace! Peace implies a harmony of affairs –

but we cannot have this harmony if we are at war with God. The good news that the Bible declares is that 'we have peace with God through our Lord Jesus Christ' (Romans 5:1). Sin and rebellion put us at war with God; the cross of Christ – by his death for our sin, when we trust the Prince of Peace in repentance and faith – brings us to peace with God. We cannot ignore the core message of Christmas and expect to benefit from it. We are at war with God, but he has sent his peacemaker.

Because of sin – envy, strife, pride and greed – war remains a reality in our fallen world. But the glory of the message of Christmas is that peace has invaded our world. Though Christ was born, like you and me, as a small baby, by his miraculous life, humble death and glorious resurrection and ascension, he was revealed as unimaginably great. Now his regenerating and restorative work of peace transforms families and even nations, both the small and the great.

Christmas means peace with God, which leads, inexorably, to peace within and the fruit of peace with others. 'In Christ' we have a new kinship – the family of God! This is the joy and peace that Christmas brings; joy because we are delivered from sin and transformed to become co-heirs with Christ, the King of creation; and peace, when we finally throw down our arms at the great armistice of the cross, for 'he himself is our peace' (Ephesians 2:14).

Revd Joe Boot is an apologist, educator, author and pastor. He serves as senior pastor of Westminster Chapel (www.westminsterchapel.ca) and founding president of the Ezra Institute for Contemporary Christianity in Toronto, Canada. Joe lives in Toronto with his wife Jenny and their three children, Naomi, Hannah and Isaac.

WHAT WILL YOU BE WEARING THIS CHRISTMAS?

David Brickner

With Hanukkah and Christmas just around the corner, many find themselves caught up in the question of clothing.

Have you pulled that gaudy Christmas sweater out of the back of your closet yet? Or maybe you are trying to figure out what kind of clothing you might buy as gifts for loved ones. Perhaps you are wondering if you're about to receive another round of socks, ties or shirts – and if so, where you will put them. Others may be fretting over what kind of fashion statement to make while attending various office parties or other events of the season.

But for just a minute I want to reflect on a very different kind of clothing, the kind the Messiah Jesus wore when he chose to be born a human being. Jesus, 'who, being in very nature God, did not consider equality with God something to be used to his own advantage; rather, he made himself nothing by taking the very nature of a servant, being made in human likeness. And being found in appearance as a man, he humbled himself ...' (Philippians 2:6–8).

The incarnation of Jesus made for a very unusual fashion statement on the world's catwalk. Jesus was 'in the form of God' – array so beautiful and breathtaking it is beyond our ability to imagine or describe. No one has seen God, but the Bible tells us that he lives in 'unapproachable light' (1 Timothy 6:16). The Bible also speaks of his magnificence in terms of the beauty of sapphires, the majesty of rainbows, of fire and sparkling brilliance. And still, these words and images give us the tiniest glimpse, a mere hint of his glorious raiment. And Jesus laid all that aside in order to don the flesh of a human being, a baby boy to be born in the dead of night in a cold, dark cave reserved for animals.

A new-born has no wardrobe; the incarnation brings Jesus into the world clothed only in the bit of blood that is present at any birth. The King of the Universe set aside majesty and beauty and power to come into this world completely naked. He had to be dressed by others. In the decision to empty himself, Y'shua chose to clothe himself with humility. This is to be the pattern and fabric for our wardrobe as well. We are told in Philippians 2:5 to 'let this mind be in you' (*King James Version*) and 1 Peter 5:5 urges us to 'be clothed with humility' (*King James Version*). Will we make that choice? What are we wearing this Christmas?

I think most of us struggle to clothe ourselves in humility. When we fail to do so, we display a certain element of spiritual immodesty. Are we embarrassed? The humility of Jesus is not our natural attire and the holiday season can become a time when that wardrobe is even less in evidence. It's so easy to lose patience in traffic, in airports, in the queue at the supermarket or with family members during the holidays. How will we choose to be different this year?

Let's remember that when he was on the earth, Jesus demonstrated humility by girding himself with a towel and washing the disciples' feet. That towel was the clothing of his servitude. I well remember Dr Vernon Grounds – who served for many years on the Jews for Jesus board of directors – teaching us about becoming members of 'the order of the towel'. In obedience to Jesus, we are to take up that metaphoric towel that symbolises the humility of serving one another.

The choice to clothe ourselves in humility carries with it profound consequences, along with incredible potential for God to work in and through us. 'Let this mind [also translated 'attitude'] be in you.' God gives us the right to choose, but reserves for himself the power to enable. We cannot be clothed with humility apart from his grace. That is why it is so important to remember the meaning of Jesus' incarnation and what it accomplished for us. Those who trust in him have been adorned with a truly wonderful wardrobe: 'For he has clothed me with garments of salvation and arrayed me in a robe of his righteousness ...' (Isaiah 61:10).

Jesus' humility became the instrument of our salvation. We can be clothed in salvation only because we have been wrapped in the robes of his righteousness. Our standing before God is not based upon our own vast intelligence or spiritual perception, but on his sovereign grace. Which is why we should wrap ourselves in humility, as he did.

Jesus not only saved us, but he served us as an example of how we might serve one another in the same humility. And not only are we to serve one another, but we are to serve the lost; because Jesus saved us we have a message of salvation to proclaim to others.

There's so much that comes to us through the grace of humility, worn as a reflection of our Saviour. Andrew Murray wrote,

> *And so Jesus came to bring humility back to earth to make us partakers of it and by it to save us. In heaven he humbled himself to become man. The humility we see in him possessed him in heaven, he brought it from there. Jesus Christ took the place and fulfilled the destiny of man as a creature by his life of perfect humility. His humility is our salvation, his salvation is our humility.*
> (Andrew Murray, *Humility*, Christian Literature Crusade, 1997)

So let us actively choose to wear garments of salvation and servitude brought to us by our Lord Jesus this season – that our spiritual wardrobe might reflect and express our loyalty to the Saviour, the one whose humble birth we celebrate.

David Brickner leads Jews for Jesus (www.jewsforjesus.org). With branches in thirteen countries including Israel, Jews for Jesus is known for its forthright evangelistic approach in major Jewish population centres around the world. David is a Jewish believer in Jesus, has been in ministry for over thirty years and has appeared many times on secular television, including the internationally syndicated programme *Larry King Live*, to make the case for Jews believing Jesus. Biblically conservative, as well as contemporary and engaging, he is a sought-after speaker for churches and conferences. He is the author of four books.

FINGERPRINTS OF GOD
Erin Clifford

What does baby Jesus, or the Christ-child, have in common with police dramas? What does the Christ, Saviour of the world, have to do with *The Bill, CSI* and – for some of the older generation – *Z Cars*? Well, the answer is: fingerprints! When we look for the evidence of who Jesus was and is, we are looking at fingerprints.

At services over the Christmas period we have readings from the Old and New Testaments. To many people, these readings may seem to be just part of a seasonal habit and chosen out of tradition, but I encourage you to put on your detective hats and look deeper, for they are all part of a file of evidence in the case for Christ.[1]

Fingerprinting in evidence didn't come about until 1910. It was a normal Saturday in September in the lives of the Hiller family who lived in Chicago, Illinois. Mr Hiller, the father of two, had just finished painting the house. It was during the night that the family was burgled. Unfortunately for him, the thief came in through the kitchen window and left three fingerprints on the window ledge in the fresh paint that Mr Hiller had just applied to the house. The police had never used fingerprinting before as a form of evidence, but here they were with evidence for the existence of a man, and now they needed to find him.

The writer of Isaiah says, 'For to us a child is born, to us a son is given, and the government will be on his shoulders. And he will be called Wonderful Counsellor, Mighty God, Everlasting Father, Prince of Peace' (Isaiah 9:6). He is writing 700 years before Jesus would be born in Bethlehem. Isaiah also writes about the virgin birth. Fingerprints – fingerprints of the Messiah to come, of what it would look like when God came in human form, with a motive of love.

In the Old Testament there are more than forty-eight major predictions of Jesus' coming. Isaiah reveals the manner of Jesus' birth (of a virgin); Micah pinpointed the place of his birth (Bethlehem); Genesis and Jeremiah specified his ancestry (a descendant of Abraham, Isaac and Jacob, from the tribe of Judah, from the house of David); the Psalms foretold his betrayal, his accusation by false witnesses, his manner of death (pierced in his hands and feet, although crucifixion hadn't been devised when the Psalms were written) and his resurrection. And on and on.

Fingerprints. And why is fingerprint evidence so important? Because the probability of two people having the same fingerprint is so inconceivable that they are considered almost infallible evidence for matching someone's identity, and the same is true for these prophecies pointing to Jesus.

For those of you who like statistics, the likelihood of just eight of these prophecies being fulfilled in one person (and remember, Jesus fulfilled all forty-eight) is one in a hundred million billion. OK, for those of us who prefer a visual illustration, it's like taking France and covering it with 50 cent pieces (two feet deep), just one single coin of which is marked. Then finding a blindfolded person and having them walk around the country and this is the probability that they will pick up that *one* coin. Those are the odds. The mathematician Peter Stoner says that the odds of all forty-eight being fulfilled in one person is one chance in a trillion, trillion, trillion, trillion, trillion (and add a further 7 trillions)!

Some might say, well, what if Jesus formed his life to fit the prophecies? Well, this could apply to a handful of the accounts, but for the majority of the predictions it would be impossible. How could he control the fact that the Sanhedrin offered Judas thirty pieces of silver to betray him? How could he arrange for his ancestry, or the place of his birth, or his method of execution, or that soldiers gambled for his clothing, or that his legs remained unbroken on the cross? How would he arrange to be born when he was?

And with this, I'll rest my 'case'. In Daniel 9:24–25, it says that Christ would appear a certain length of time after King Artaxerxes I issued a decree for the Jewish people to go from Persia to rebuild the walls of Jerusalem. That puts the anticipated appearance of the Messiah at the exact moment in history when Jesus did show up! Fingerprints.

So, let me leave you with this thought. When you look at the baby Jesus, and sing the carols, don't just see a fulfilled prophecy or a man identified by the fingerprints in history, but see his motive for the whole thing. God entered humanity out of love. 'God becoming man, spirit taking on flesh, the infinite entering the finite, the eternal becoming time-bound'[2] … out of love.

> *How silently, how silently, the wondrous gift is given!*
> *So God imparts to human hearts the blessings of his heaven.*
> *No ear may hear his coming; but in this world of sin,*
> *Where meek souls will receive him still, the dear Christ enters in.*

And my Christmas prayer is that we all might with sincerity of heart respond … 'O come to us, abide with us, our Lord Emmanuel.'

Revd Erin Clifford is on the staff at Holy Trinity Brompton in London, and is also tutor in Preaching at St Mellitus College. She received her Masters of Divinity from Gordon-Conwell Theological Seminary in Boston USA, after five years of urban ministry in Washington, DC. Originally from the USA, Erin came to London on a one-year Preaching Fellowship. She has a BA in Speech Communication and is ordained in the Church of England.

---

[1] The statistics included in this sermon come from Lee Strobel, *The Case for Christmas: A Journalist Investigates the Identity of the Child in the Manger,* Zondervan, 2005.

[2] Lee Strobel, *The Case for Christmas*, p.59.

THE GOD WHO WORKS FROM BACK TO FRONT
Bayless Conley

Born in Bethlehem, went into Egypt, ended up in Nazareth – that it might be fulfilled which was spoken by the prophet: he will be born in Bethlehem, I called my Son out of Egypt, and he shall be a Nazarene.

Looking back on that, you think, 'God, your plan is amazing, the way that it unfolded.' But, you know, it's only by looking *back* that that was able to be discerned, not going forward.

Think about Joseph. He and Mary have to travel over sixty miles to get to Bethlehem. And she's not just a little pregnant, she's way pregnant! Sixty miles of Joseph leading her on a donkey – or maybe she was sitting in some handmade wooden cart with wooden wheels. No shock absorbers. It felt every bump and every rut in the road. Every rock jarred her. That trip, which took days and days over rough, rocky dirt roads, was not fun. It must have been horrendous! And on top of that, Joseph and Mary didn't have a lot of money. They spend days, maybe sleeping out in the open at night, and they finally get there, and Joseph tries to get a place in the inn because his pregnant wife is just about ready to deliver, and they say, 'There is no room for you!' And Joseph had to be saying, 'God, why are you letting this happen?'

Somebody says, 'Well, there's a stable down here.' And Joseph is thinking, 'A stable? A smelly, dirty stable? God, what's going on? I thought that having this child was going to be blessed by you. What am I going to do? God, where are you?'

You see, Joseph wasn't thinking, 'I was wondering how you were going to get us to Bethlehem so that this prophecy could be fulfilled.'

He couldn't see it, looking forward. Looking forward it seemed hard and wrong and confusing and maybe even cruel. Only by looking backwards could it be fully understood that God actually used a world ruler and shifted the whole world around. Caesar says, 'You know what? I have an idea. We're going to take a census, and we're going to do something new. I want to find out how many people are in my empire. But everybody's got to go back to the town they were born in. I want everyone to go back to where their lineage springs from, and that's where we are going to take the census.' And if Caesar says it, you dare not disobey.

And, looking back, we go, 'God, amazing! You used this selfish, prideful world ruler, and you shifted people all over the world to bring to pass your plan.' I'll guarantee you Joseph was *not* thinking, 'Amazing!'

And then they went into Egypt. To Joseph, it looks like things are getting worse. Not, 'I wondered how you were going to get us down here and fulfil that prophecy. Imagine thinking of using an insane, murderous king to fulfil your plan! Fantastic!' No, he couldn't have seen it at all, going forward. The Bible said he was afraid. Only by looking back could he, and we, discern the unfolding of God's amazing plan. Going through it, it just looked like trouble, trouble and more trouble.

The Bible declares that God makes known the end from the beginning (Isaiah 46:10). Nothing takes him by surprise. And that's why 'we know that in all things God works for the good of those who love him, who have been called according to his purpose' (Romans 8:28). That means our mistakes, our failures, world events … he weaves his plan through it all.

Maybe you've had a very hard year. Maybe you've been in an extremely difficult season, and you're thinking, 'God, what's happening? Why? Where are you?' Going forward, we can't see it all. And though God does not cause the bad things to happen – I would like to emphasise that – he is not taken by surprise when they do happen. And he can be trusted. Trust him. Going forward, you may not be able to see; but, looking back, there will come a point when you say, 'Well, I didn't see you at all, but I see that was connected to that; and because that happened, this happened.' And, looking back, you can see God working through all the stuff. It never took *him* by surprise, though you may not have seen his hand at all.

I remember when I first moved up to Oregon. I had some pretty major league problems with drug addiction and some other things and decided I needed to get out of the neighbourhood or I was going to end up in an early grave. I thought I'd try college and I looked at a number of different universities. I was accepted at several and went and checked several of them out and there were a number of them that were just perfect, everything that I wanted. But there was a little college in Southern Oregon that was, actually, the last on the list. But something spoke to me. And at the time I remember sensing it, like, 'I don't know what this is, but I feel like I'm supposed to go here.' And so I did. On my first day there on campus I heard someone call my name. It was a drug dealer I knew from Long Beach. And I was right back down the slide again. But it was there in Southern Oregon that a 12-year-old boy came up to me in a park and told me about Jesus Christ. It was the first time in my life I heard the gospel. And, looking back, I recognise now what it was that spoke to me. It was the Holy Spirit. And in retrospect, I see God's plan.

You see, looking backwards, you can see the plan of God – not always going forward. And I want to tell you: God has been working for you. Trust him, especially when you don't understand and when you cannot see him doing anything.

Pastor Bayless Conley leads Cottonwood Church, a thriving church located in Orange County, California (www.cottonwood.org). His television programme, *Answers with Bayless Conley,* airs in over 100 nations worldwide. A frequent conference speaker, Bayless is known for his clear, practical presentation of the gospel. Consistently fresh insights mark his proclamation of God's truth, and his messages bring the life-changing truth of God's Word into everyday lives. Bayless and his wife, Janet, are the parents of three grown children. Together they passionately pursue life, family, ministry and their relationship with Jesus Christ.

NAME ABOVE ALL NAMES
Gavin Collins

This is how the birth of Jesus came about:

The night was cold and CHRISp, and Mary and Joseph had gone to Bethlehem to register for the census. The town was so full that they couldn't find anywhere to stay, but right at the edge of the village, just as the path began to PETER out, they came to a small, dingy stable. It was very RICKety and dilapidated and, as the Americans would say, it didn't even have a JOHN! It really was fit for neither woman NOR MAN, but Mary and Joseph were so desperate that ANNIE old place would do. Joseph said to Mary: 'I know the RUTH is really low, but if EILEEN like this, I can just fit in.' They couldn't afford to pay a FI-ONA said that as it was just a stable he wouldn't charge them even a few BOB. Joseph agreed, and as the door was LUC-Y went in. That night the time came for Mary to have her baby, and she laid him in the manger.

There were some shepherds out in the fields, who suddenly heard a RUSSELL and saw an angel standing there. The angel said to the shepherds: 'I bring you some news that's JUST IN – this very night in Bethlehem a baby has been born who will be Christ the Lord!' And suddenly the sound of a CAROL filled the night sky, a choir of angels singing: 'GLORIA in excelsis!'

'GORDON Bennett!' the shepherds said: 'To think that God could have told this great news to any old TOM, DICK or HARRY, and yet he's chosen to tell it to us, by GEORGE! – SHIRLEY we'd better go straight down to Bethlehem to see this wonderful sight.'

Meanwhile, in the city of Jerusalem, some strange travellers had come to see the king. 'We come from A-LANd far away,' said the Wise Men. 'We saw a new star in the east and we realised it meant that a new king has been born so we decided to SALLY forth and follow it. The journey was long and hard: it was a bit like GULLIVER's Travels, and there was certainly no THOMAS Cook shop to help us book it! We've been BOBbing along, up and down mountains and across SANDY deserts, and now the star's brought us to Jerusalem to see the new king.'

'For PETE's sake!' exploded Herod. 'Are you taking the MICKEY? – A new king born in my land, you've got to be JOE-king! I won't have it. I'll take legal action – I'll SUE!'

'JACK it in,' replied the shepherds. 'Keep your AARON! Do you know that when you're angry, your face goes all wonky?' 'Yes, one IS-AIAH than the other!'

Herod asked his advisors: 'Where will the promised king be born?' They replied: "Hang on a MO-SES here that it will be in Bethlehem of Judea, so that's the place TO-BY sure.'

Herod told the Wise Men where to go: 'LUKE very carefully, and WEN-DY star comes to rest, that will MARK the place where the baby has been BJORN.' He tried to appear friendly as he gave them a PAT on the back and said to them: 'After you've seen the new king, WILL you come back and tell me so that I, too, can worship him?' But the Wise Men didn't trust Herod. 'I BETTY's up to no good,' they said, so they went back by another way in CASIE found out, and as they disappeared without a TRACE-Y didn't know where to look. Herod was livid when he realised he'd been tRICKed.

The Wise Men entered the stable and saw the baby lying in the manger. The baby was a real bundle of JOY – a gift of GRACE who would bring HOPE to the world. The Wise Men CARRIEd strange gifts for the baby – precious jewels, strange spices ANNA unusual fragrance. 'That's a strange smell,' said Mary. 'Is it JASMINE?' 'No, it's FRANKincense.' And their main gift was very precious – not just AMBER or RUBY, but gold!

After they'd given their presents, the Wise Men felt that they should NEIL down in front of this new-born king. 'What's his name?' they asked Mary and Joseph.

And Mary looked up and smiled and replied: 'He's got the name that is above all names: He's called "Jesus", which means, "God saves".'

This is the Word of the Lord. Thanks be to God.

Ven. Gavin Collins trained as a solicitor before being ordained in the Church of England. He ministered for fourteen years in parish ministry in Cambridge and Chorleywood. He is currently the Archdeacon of the Meon in Portsmouth Diocese, where he is responsible for the care and support of fifty-five churches in South East Hampshire (www.portsmouth.anglican.org). Gavin is committed to seeing the growth of God's Kingdom through proclamation, worship, fellowship and building loving communities that are externally focused to embrace those around them. Gavin is married to Christina, a practice nurse, and they have three school-aged children. He is a life-long supporter of Brighton and Hove Albion FC, which teaches him many lessons about what it means to live as a man of faith!

CHRISTMAS IN A NUTSHELL!
Jodie Collins

Here we are again, that time of year, who can believe it? Have you got the tree and all the decorations up? Have you even thought about it yet? (I haven't!) Have you done your Christmas shopping already? Have you even started? (I haven't!) Can you remember a present you received last year? Or the best present? The worst present? Last year I gave my brother a gift called 'Nothing' and my dad got a toy called Joey the JCB because he likes building projects!

But what Christmas is really about, in a *nutshell*, is that ... God showed up! It's not really about the shopping, the tree or the presents. It's about the fact that God – Creator of the universe, the one who scattered the stars by hand – cared enough about us to put himself on this earth as a tiny baby.

> *When the time came, he set aside the privileges of deity and took on the status of a slave, became human! Having become human, he stayed human. It was an incredibly humbling process. He didn't claim special privileges. Instead, he lived a selfless, obedient life and then died a selfless, obedient death.* (Philippians 2, *The Message*)

Still, I've been thinking about carol services ... they are really very odd! They are popular occasions, with readings about the birth of Jesus and popular carols; and sometimes there is candlelight to capture the atmosphere and wonder as we celebrate the birth of our Saviour. The most well-known form of carol service is the 'Festival of Nine Lessons and Carols'. This was actually introduced in 1880 by a clergyman in Truro and was conducted at 10 p.m. on Christmas Eve to get men out of the pubs early so that they would not be drunk at midnight Mass!

Every year we tell and hear the same story: Mary and Joseph; donkey; innkeeper says no; stable; baby born; angels; shepherds and sheep; star of Bethlehem; wise men; gifts; the end (my paraphrase!). It is a good job we have the readings. And there is now even something on Twitter called the Natwivity, which tells the story of the birth of Jesus through tweets!

When we celebrate birthdays we don't usually retell the story of the person's birth at their party; we don't recall details of the pregnancy or the thoughts and feelings of Mum and Dad when they heard they were going to have a baby. Yet, every Christmas, we sing carols about Jesus' birth and retell all the 'baby-talk' details that have been passed down to us. Lots of my friends have had babies recently and I've heard a lot of pregnancy and birth stories – to be honest, I've heard my fair share. There's nothing I couldn't tell you about pregnancy and birth and each set of parents' stories about how they felt and what happened – but thank goodness I only have to hear each story once. Hopefully we won't be gathering every year to hear the story all over again.

When I have a 'significant' birthday I can't see us all sitting around, talking about how Mum and Dad hadn't been surprised by me turning up, that they'd planned it and were very excited as they got ready for my arrival. And then going through the details of how I arrived a week early, they rushed to the clinic, and at 5.50 a.m. – after telling us all the details of the breach birth – I arrived weighing only 5lbs. Then there is the tale of how my brother came to visit me but he really wanted Mum and Dad to take home the jaundiced baby with bandages round his head, he wasn't so keen on me. Telling that story every year could become very dull …

So is it odd that we choose to come to a carol service and hear about Jesus' birth every year? Why do we do that? We do it because there's more to it than remembering a baby being born, and us all giving each other gifts to celebrate his birthday. In a nutshell, it's about God seeing the mess of this world and getting involved … God showed up.

I've heard it said that:

> *If our greatest need had been information,*
> *God would have sent us an educator;*
>
> *If our greatest need had been technology,*
> *God would have sent us a scientist;*
>
> *If our greatest need had been money,*
> *God would have sent us an economist;*
>
> *If our greatest need had been pleasure,*
> *God would have sent us an entertainer;*
>
> *But our greatest need was forgiveness,*
> *so God sent us a Saviour.*

(Source unknown)

And when we crack a nutshell open, that's what it's about.

So many of us only think of Jesus in the manger. It's a great place to start but there's more to it than a cute baby lying in a bed of straw! It's about a God stepping down from heaven to meet our deepest need.

Jodie Collins lives in London, where she heads up the charity Beyond Ourselves, working alongside local churches in Zambia helping to build and develop community schools (www.beyondourselves.co.uk). As well as being a speaker and evangelist, Jodie was previously a teacher, and also ministered in the nightlife area of Tenerife for four years.

WHAT WOULD JESUS SAY TO SANTA CLAUS?

Mark Conner

Have you noticed that Santa Claus has gradually been taking centre stage at Christmas of late and that Jesus has been forced to take more of a back seat? Who is this Santa guy and where did he come from anyway?

Christmas is the most widely celebrated holiday in the Western world. It was Pope Gregory who established 25 December as the supposed birth of Christ; 'Christmas' literally means 'mass of Christ'. Christians after the time of Constantine co-opted a number of pagan festivals, adding Christian elements to them. To the December winter solstice, and various harvest festivities, they added a Nativity crib and the singing of Christmas carols. Eventually, the Santa Claus image emerged – with sledge, reindeer and a sack of toys. It was an American invention that first appeared in an 1868 drawing. However, the Father Christmas legend was based at least in part on a much earlier story of a fourth-century bishop by the name of Saint Nicholas.

So anyway … what would Jesus say to Santa Claus? Here's what I think he might say:

Firstly, I think Jesus would say, **'Thanks for encouraging the spirit of giving.'** Yes, I think Jesus would have something positive to say to Santa Claus. We live in a world of increasing selfishness and greed. Christmas is a time when we think more about others, which is a good thing. God is a great giver (John 3:16) – that's why he sent Jesus – and he delights when we become generous like him

(Matthew 10:8; 2 Corinthians 9:7). Like God, we all need to adopt more of a giving attitude in life, as well as one of gratitude, affirmation and encouragement.

Secondly, I think Jesus might say, **'True fulfilment is not found in things.'** Santa's focus at this time of year is based on a belief that more things will make people happier. But people need more than mere things. Things may be nice but ultimately they are empty and they never fully satisfy (see Luke 12:15). We need the love, peace and joy that only God can provide through a relationship with him and with other people. Love people and use things – not the other way around.

Thirdly, I think Jesus would say, **'Good works aren't enough.'** Santa's game is one of getting rewarded for what you do – for being nice rather than naughty. The truth is that none of us are ever good enough. Our efforts fall short (Romans 3:23). That's why Jesus came: to live and then to die for our shortcomings, and then to offer us eternal life, as a free gift, not as a reward for our good deeds. Christmas is not about what we have done but about what God has done for us … in Christ (Ephesians 2:8–10).

Fourthly, I think Jesus might say, **'You're not the reason for the season.'** Christmas is about Christ. Jesus came to earth as the Saviour of world. He is the eternal Son of God who arrived on earth 2,000 years ago. Santa Claus is a recent addition, an 'add-on'. This celebration isn't about him. Jesus Christ is the most influential person in history. We mark time by his very arrival. Jesus is the 'hinge of history'. Let's keep the 'Christ' in Christmas. Remember, he *is* the real reason for the season!

Finally, Jesus might say, **'You're not real, but I am.'** Santa Claus is a figment of people's imagination, a mythical hero. Sorry, kids, but Santa isn't real (parents, ease it to them slowly!). He's merely a character – like Mickey Mouse or Buzz Lightyear. Jesus is real. You can't see him but he is alive. He is not a myth or a legend or an imaginary person. He is not only real, but he'll be back. However, his second coming won't be like his first coming. He will come in power and glory and every eye will see him.

Can you see that the gospel of Jesus is quite different from the gospel of Santa Claus? Where's your faith? In Santa Claus or in

Jesus Christ? Jesus is knocking at the door of your heart. Do you have room for him? I believe that he is the true and living God, the Prince of Peace, the Saviour of the world, offering us forgiveness and real life. Turn to him and place your faith in him today. Follow him and live for him.

Christians: don't picket Santa Claus. Don't become an old scrooge or a humbug Christian. Just because Santa is an anagram for Satan does *not* mean that he is the devil! Jesus Christ is the true meaning of Christmas. Let's bring him back to centre stage!

Pastor Mark Conner is the Senior Minister of CityLife Church,
a diverse community of Christ-followers meeting in multiple locations
in Melbourne, Australia (www.citylifechurch.com). Mark has a genuine
love for people and a passion to help them grow and change. He has
a Doctor of Ministry degree from Fuller Theological Seminary. Mark is
married to Nicole and they have three young adult children.
For more information, see www.markconner.com.au
(www.twitter.com/MarkAConner).

11

INDESCRIBABLE!
Anthony Delaney

I want to focus in on just one verse from the Bible – 2 Corinthians 9:15, 'Thanks be to God for his INDESCRIBABLE GIFT!' That word *indescribable* is only used once in the whole Bible, right there. But I have been thinking, how many times have I tried to describe this indescribable gift since the day I first opened it myself, 25 years ago. And if I live another 25 years and you come to hear me then, I'll still be trying to describe it! And I won't have run out of superlatives by then.

This verse was written by a man called Paul. He just stopped in the middle of a letter he was writing to a church to encourage them to be generous one day, and added that line in – because he was so overwhelmed by God's generosity.

Now Paul is not saying here, 'You shouldn't describe it ...' He's saying, 'You can't.' You can't fully describe God's free grace and abundant love – how sinful people get a personal relationship and peace with a righteous God, by having their sins forgiven and their judgement removed. How they get power to change and be healed. How you can get the deepest longings of your heart satisfied by the one who made your heart. You can't describe all that.

The world today is full of preachers trying to! It's good to *try* to describe it and I love to hear what we call testimonies. Before they're going to be baptised you'll hear people say, 'I'll tell you what it feels like for me ... the change God's love has made – it was like a weight lifted off me, like this joy came inside ... like the world went from black and white to colour.' They'll say, 'It was like I could forgive people who'd hurt me …' 'Like I suddenly had HOPE …' They'll say, 'I can't describe how good God's been to me, how good it is to know Jesus …'

It's indescribable! Paul uses a Greek word – *anekdiageto*. It means 'beyond description', as in, 'Words fail me …'

Have you ever had that moment when something takes your breath away and you say, 'Well, I don't know what to say!' 'It's so good, I can't *tell you*!' 'I run out of superlatives … it's the best!' Maybe you got a present that's really good this year? But Paul is talking about a better present. Beyond the greatest. And notice, it really is a *gift*. It's *free*. It comes from God!

What is God's indescribable gift? Some people I read, as I researched that little word, said, 'It is the gift of salvation.' Others think, 'It is the gift of Jesus Christ.' I say, why not both? You can't separate the two actually – because the Bible says that apart from Jesus there is no salvation! That's why he came. That's what his name means. 'God to the rescue!' It's all wrapped up in him. God's most precious gift, all wrapped up in Jesus, all wrapped up in a manger. The Bible says there's *no other name* given by which we can be saved. Salvation is given to us in Jesus Christ.

It makes my head spin when I try to look at the heavens and grasp how huge it is. That's something else way beyond my comprehension. If the universe is indescribably vast, the God who made it all must be indescribably great. The Bible says, 'In the beginning, God created the heavens and the earth' (Genesis 1:1). But for some people, that just makes him feel more and more removed, and makes them question, 'Doesn't that mean he's so distant – how can I know him?' If that's you – Jesus is the answer. Because the Bible *also* says, 'In the beginning was the Word, and the Word was with God, and the Word was God. He was with God in the beginning. Through him all things were made; without him nothing was made that has been made … The Word became flesh and made his dwelling among us … full of grace and truth' (John 1:1–3,14). Christmas is when we celebrate that God has come to us – and that he became flesh – human.

Did you know that Jesus said to his disciples, 'Anyone who has seen me has seen the Father' (John 14:9)? Jesus is God reaching out to us. This is the good news that got the angels so excited that first Christmas: God wants to be known. He wants to be loved. He wants to be a Father and a Friend. He wants to remove every barrier that stops you being everything he made you to be. You can know God – just as personally as you know anyone in this world.

You may say that you don't deserve that – but Jesus is a gift. Salvation is a gift. We don't earn it. We receive Jesus; we receive salvation exactly as we'd receive a gift. If we earn it, it is not a gift. That's why, when the apostle Paul starts thinking about what Jesus means to him personally, what Jesus has done for him and what he's going to do in history and in the world including you and me, he says, 'Thanks be to God, for this free gift – the best gift ever – so good, I can't describe it ...'

No matter what gifts we give, they pale in comparison with what God gave us that first Christmas Day. 'For God so loved the world that *he gave his one and only Son*, that whoever believes in him shall not perish but have eternal life' (John 3:16). The gift of Jesus, the gift of forgiveness, salvation, relationship with God – it's beyond words. How can you fully explain it? I can't, you can't – it is indescribable! But you can know whether you've received it.

How do you know you've received this gift from God? Because you're grateful and you say thank you!

Revd Anthony Delaney leads Ivy Manchester, a growing and dynamic church in the city he served for ten years as a plain clothes policeman. The church meets in a monastery, cinemas, malls, night clubs and even a church building (www.ivymanchester.org). Anthony speaks at various national conferences, such as New Wine, and regularly broadcasts on BBC Radio 5 Live and Radio 4. His book, *Diamond Geezers* (Integrity Media Europe, 2011), is helping men discover what it really means to have nothing to prove, nothing to hide and everything to live for. For more information, see www.anthonydelaney.com.

THE QUEEN'S SPEECH
Greg Downes

Christmas wouldn't be Christmas without the Queen's speech. Having opened the presents, and replete from our Christmas dinners, we settle down to watch our beloved head of state's take on the passing year, before falling asleep in the chair or watching a movie.

Nicholas Witchell commented that the Queen's 2011 speech was 'deeply spiritual' and it's perhaps not surprising that the media should find this noteworthy because for many people in the UK Christmas has become a secular festival.

Since Christmas is here to stay I would argue that we need to seize the opportunity it offers us to share the good news that love has indeed come down at Christmas in the person of Jesus Christ – the world needs a stable influence!

CHRISTmas starts with Christ

A reading commonly used at Christmas is John 1:1–14. It speaks of the mystery of the incarnation, the doctrine of God becoming a human being. Jesus Christ is none other than God with skin on. This passage teaches us three things about Christmas that tend to get lost beneath the wrapping paper and tinsel:

1. Jesus can be trusted because of who he is

John takes us back first to the dawn of creation itself and then to the first Christmas when the agent of creation, the eternal Word of God, enters our world in human form. If this man Jesus is 'the Word' then the inescapable truth is that *in the beginning was Jesus, Jesus was with God and Jesus was God.* If Jesus is God we can trust him totally.

There are many things we put our faith and confidence in that are not worthy of them, but we can put our faith and confidence in Jesus Christ because of who he is, because he is none other than the Son of the living God.

2. Jesus gives two kinds of life

Verses 3 and 4 state that 'through him [Jesus] all things were made; without him nothing was made that has been made. In him was life, and that life was the light of all mankind.' Jesus Christ gives us not one but *two* kinds of life. You have already received one of them, the second you may not have received. One is automatic and innate, the other is conditional and needs appropriating. While we have only one word for *life* in English there are more in Greek (the language of the New Testament). One is *bios* (from which we get the word biology), and that's life in terms of physical life. This is the kind of life that you have by virtue of the fact that you are reading this sermon! Another is *zoe* (from which the word zoology is derived), and that's life in terms of spiritual life. This is the kind of life that is conditional and needs appropriating – if you have it it's because you have exercised your will to receive it.

The fact that you are alive today – have biological life – is because of Jesus, 'through him all things were made'. It is his gift to *you*. But in verse 4 – 'In him was life, and that life was the light of all mankind' – the word used is *zoe*, spiritual life, supernatural life, a type of life that can bring illumination to the human race.

I used to be a prison chaplain and one morning the officers were a bit short staffed, so asked me to accompany one of the inmates back to his cell. As I was escorting David, aged 17, I sensed a word of knowledge from God about him – a fact about this young man that I couldn't possibly have known. I spoke it out: 'David, were you tempted to commit suicide last night … about 9 o'clock? I believe God would say to you, "I am the author of life and I created you to know me and to walk in my ways."' David began to sob as we got to his cell and he began to tell me his story.

He had been admitted to the prison the day before, having never been to prison before, and he was really scared. He was afraid he would be bullied or beaten up and ended up feeling desperate and looking for a way out. The night before, he had been watching TV in the association room and when a particular programme finished he had asked if he could go back to his cell. Back in his cell he began to think of a way to end his life. There were two things in his cell – a brown book and a pen. He picked up the pen and wondered if there was any way that he could sharpen it and use it as a weapon to kill himself but decided it would be hugely painful and wouldn't work. He then picked up the brown book – which was a Gideon Bible – opened it at random and read a few lines, then he said a prayer before trying to get to sleep as an anaesthetic. 'I know it was 9 o'clock, because that was the time the TV programme finished and I came back to the cell.' Perhaps not surprisingly, David was keen to know more about this God who knew his innermost thoughts and cared about him so much and I prayed with him that day and he surrendered his life to Jesus Christ.

The next day I went to visit David. He wasn't expecting me but I found him sitting on his bed, reading the Bible. When he saw me he grinned – he looked totally different from the dejected young man I'd encountered just twenty-four hours earlier. He was reading a bit in Acts about the apostle Paul being flogged and exclaimed, 'Oh, it's nothing – what we've got to put up with in here – compared to what those Christians put up with.'

David's life had become so painful that he had wanted to take his own life (*bios*). As he turned to Jesus Christ, he received new life (*zoe*), a supernatural, spiritual life that began to transform his whole being.

3. Christ is the gift that God can't wait to give

John 1:12 states: 'Yet to all who did receive him, to those who believed in his name, he gave the right to become children of God.'

It was with an exhortation to appropriate this new spiritual (zoe) life that the Queen finished her Christmas Day speech in 2011. I will leave the last word to Her Majesty: 'It is my prayer that on this

Christmas Day we might all find room in our lives for the message of the angels and for the love of God through Christ our Lord.'

Revd Greg Downes is the Director of the Centre for Missional Leadership, the second campus of the London School of Theology (www.lst.ac.uk/cml). A native of Lancaster, Greg moved to London to study for a degree in Social Policy and Administration before completing a PGCE in Religious Education at Cambridge University. After teaching in London and then working as John Stott's study assistant he read Theology at Oxford University before ordination in the Church of England. Since then, Greg has been a curate, prison chaplain, theological college lecturer and university chaplain. He is theologian-in-residence for *Christianity* magazine and a regular speaker at mission events and conferences.

REFOCUSING THE LENS OF CHRISTMAS
Alison Fenning

In 722 BC the prophet Isaiah spoke a promise of a Messiah who would come from the throne and passion of the Almighty.

Introduction

The Christmas season gives us an opportunity to reflect on the activity of God in sending his Son Jesus Christ into the world. For some, the lens of Christmas is faulty. While we may enjoy the traditions of gift giving, carols, food and family gathering, we have not thought deeply about the birth of Christ and the impact it makes on our lives and communities today.

Imagine the Kingdom of heaven as the base of heavenly activity, a mission base getting ready to launch the most powerful person, God's Son, whose birth would change the shape of all creation for ever. The Christ is about to be born – the One who was promised 722 years earlier by the Almighty God, through his chosen mouth-piece the prophet Isaiah.

Through the Messiah the whole of creation will be able to enter into eternal living and relationship with God the Father and be saved from all wickedness and judgement. Hope has now come – an opportunity to be free from all that seeks to dull and destroy life, if we choose to receive the gift of heaven. Those who follow Christ and respond to the gift of heaven will be fully reconciled to the Father. Through his life and death the resurrection of all humanity will be made possible and the Kingdom of God will be ushered in, to reveal the true glory, goodness and all-powerfulness of the one known as God.

Today we sometimes view our world as an unsafe place to live in. We all face many unknowns every day, just as the people did in the time of Isaiah and also when Jesus was born. Isaiah reassures us that the coming of the Messiah was a result of God's zealousness towards us. He was and still is passionate about us and wants us to turn our hearts towards him. Here is an A, B and C that may be a helpful tool for us this Christmas season, to refocus our lens and feel the presence of hope as Isaiah and Mary did.

Activity

With God, Kingdom activity is always at hand. In Luke we hear about how Mary was visited by an angel and told how it would happen – the coming of the Messiah promised 722 years earlier is fulfilled. The promises of Almighty God come to pass.

Our reflection may be directed towards the fact that God is faithful and trustworthy: what he says happens. If that is so, why wouldn't we receive the gift of heaven, wanting to be part of a Kingdom full of promise and hope, whose King's footprints are full of justice and righteousness as opposed to the destructive world of the unrighteous, where only death and unknowns are the footprints?

The little baby born into the manger is King Jesus, who brought hope and redeemed creation through his life and death. Echoes of hope sounded around his birth. We must seek to be joined into his Kingdom for he is the way, the truth and the life as was promised. Activity stimulates our reflection.

Belief

By the end of a year we have all been through some good and some not-so-good things. Our hearts and minds have been reshaped by our experience.

Even though we read that she feared, Mary accepted the future that God had in mind for her. She humbled herself under the hand of God and her soul was restored from fear so that she had hope in her heart. Hope is described in the Bible as full confidence in what we know to be true. It is not wishful thinking. Mary had full confidence as she received the promise of God. Can we stand back from the experiences of this last year and once again focus on God's promises and the confidence they bring? As we seek to find Jesus and the meaning of Christmas can we trust him with our lives, believing that he can change our fear into faith? Believing brings restoration.

Commitment

Humanity searches for God around the Christmas season, asking, 'Is there more to life? What does it mean to become a follower of Jesus Christ?' We listen to the stories shared through the Nativity plays, films and books and try to understand.

John 3:16 reminds us that Christ was born with a heavenly purpose, to liberate humanity and creation from the curse of death and destruction. If we acknowledge our own wickedness and turn from such things, accepting that Jesus Christ was born to die as the Saviour of the world, we will be saved from judgement, oppression and eternal death. The curse that came on the world through sin has been reversed though Jesus Christ, who obeyed and died on a tree – his mission commitment to us and to God Almighty (Romans 5:12–21).

God is committed to us and provided an everlasting gift, his Son, through whom we can be restored to a right relationship with the Father. We move from living in the unknown to living in the known promises and purposes of God for our lives. A truly supernatural change occurs. Commitment produces resurrection.

Conclusion

Jesus had a relationship with God Almighty in which he would speak to him and listen to him. He gave up his life and lived to please the Father, even suffering obedience in death so we might have life and be free!

In John 14:23, Jesus made a promise: 'Anyone who loves me will obey my teaching. My Father will love them, and we will come to them and make our home with them.' The resurrected Christ, God Almighty and the Holy Spirit will come to live with us. We are not left as orphans or abandoned but are in a relationship, just as Jesus was when he was alive. When Christ comes and dwells in our hearts we walk and live in resurrection power. The same power that lifted Jesus from the grave lives in us, granting us freedom to be obedient.

Response

The Christmas story still impacts the world today. How will we respond? We can go back to the cute story and enjoy all the traditions that the season brings or we can embrace it as a life-changing opportunity to reconnect with God, through accepting and recognising the true meaning of Christmas. Choose the real gift giver this season and have a new start. Santa's gifts are not everlasting but God, who put the plan of making a way back to himself into action by giving the gift of his Son, is. The lens that was faulty has now been refocused and we can see the meaning of the season.

Alison Fenning works with the RSVP Trust (www.rsvptrust.co.uk). She is a passionate and inspiring speaker and evangelist with a compelling story to tell. Based in the UK and married to Richard she is a frequent traveller internationally, investing in leaders and the vulnerable.

THE PROBLEM WITH CHRISTMAS!
Mark Greenwood

Christmas is a fantastic time of year but it's not without its problems. I remember reading about a house that had 250,000 Christmas lights. The problem was that the drain on their electricity was so great that they couldn't boil their kettle! Sometimes in the exuberance of the celebration there lies a problem.

The problem of over-indulging

My friend had more people coming round for Christmas lunch than usual. He went looking for a turkey and was looking through the frozen section but couldn't find one big enough, so he asked one of the extra Christmas staff, 'Do these turkeys get any bigger?' 'No, Sir,' was the reply, 'they're dead.'

It is a pressure making sure that the Christmas dinner works perfectly and making sure that everyone has enough – but the truth is we all eat far too much at Christmas. You know the feeling when you have eaten more than your body can take. 'Never again' are the usual words – that is, until next Christmas when we do the same thing again! We eat too much turkey, pudding, mince pies and nuts and drink too much. The only exercise we get is when we change channels on the TV! The average person will gain six pounds in weight over Christmas.

There are 180 calories in an average mince pie and it takes forty-five minutes of continual hoovering to burn them off! During the 1640s and 1650s there were a number of Acts of Parliament authorising the imprisonment of anyone found guilty of breaking the fast days by indulging in rich food and although at the Restoration of the monarchy all ordinances and acts passed during the 1640s and 1650s were overturned, stories still circulate each year to the effect that eating mince pies is illegal on Christmas Day!

But Christmas is not about gaining weight, it's about losing what weighs us down. The Bible says, 'Cast all your anxiety on him because he cares for you' (1 Peter 5:7). Whatever concerns or worries you may have this Christmas – bring them to God.

The problem of overspending

In the rush of last-minute Christmas shopping a woman bought a box of fifty identical greetings cards. Without bothering to read the verse, she hastily signed and addressed all but one of them. Several days after she had posted them, she came across the one card that hadn't been sent. She looked at the message she had sent and was horrified to read: 'This card is just to say a little gift is on the way.'

We can spend without really thinking and the average family will spend £1,000 on food for Christmas. A few years ago Visa posted an advertisement that read, 'The good news this Christmas is that we have cut the interest on our card.' But the good news this Christmas is the same good news of every Christmas – 'God so loved the world that he gave his one and only Son, that whoever believes in him shall not perish but have eternal life' (John 3:16).

Christmas is not about getting into debt, it's about God getting us out of debt. God spent exactly what needed to be spent on that first Christmas night – not on the stable but on your life: he gave all he had.

The problem of over too quickly

Christmas doesn't last very long and yet what happened on that first Christmas was, and is, long-lasting.

'You are to give him the name Jesus, because he will save his people from their sins' (Matthew 1:21). The clue is in the name. Jesus was sent as God's rescue plan for our world – and that includes you. Jesus wants to rescue you from a life without God.

The best way to make Christmas work is the best way to make life work. Give it all over to God, acknowledging your need of him and starting an amazing journey that won't be over in just a few days.

Revd Mark Greenwood has been a full-time evangelist for twenty-four years. He is married to Emma and has two children, Robin and Nathalie. He is the director of The Forty Three Trust, an organisation that helps churches to communicate the message of Christianity in a way that people can understand (www.fortythreetrust.com). He draws on his stand-up comedy experience to make his talks entertaining as well as clear.

SHOULD CHRISTMAS BE BANNED?
Greg Haslam

One Christmas, a high-street department store ordered posters for their shop windows to boost their sales. Unfortunately, the printer made an error over one crucial letter and passers-by read, 'WE *FAKE* A GREAT INTEREST IN ALL OF OUR CUSTOMERS!' In some Yuletide businesses that's not very far from the truth. No wonder there's a surge of cynicism as each Christmas approaches.

The Christmas panto is a major feature of the festive season in Britain and celebrities, cheery songs, really villanous villains and 'He's behind you!' audience participation are all part of the fun. Herod the Great was one such monstrous villain, and he wanted to stop Christmas when it had barely begun. Every year we see evidence that at least some people think 'Enough is enough!' when it comes to Christmas. In recent years, town councillors have banned Christmas tree lights on a town-square Christmas tree on the grounds of 'Health and Safety', and companies have stopped staff Christmas parties and mistletoe hanging to prevent drink-induced sexual harrassment cases. In some parts of the UK public references to 'Christmas' have been outlawed for fear of offending 'ethnic minorities'. This raises questions: 'Is Christmas really so bad for our health?', 'What could possibly be so offensive about celebrating the birth of a baby?' and 'Is Christmas really beyond its sell-by date?'

King Herod could be the patron saint of all such kill-joys! His behaviour seems to have been consistently insecure, paranoid, irrational and homicidal. His emotions over the news of the Messiah's birth left him in a rage (Matthew 2:3–8,16–18) and we may ask, 'What is wrong with him?', and *all* modern kill-joys for that matter? Is there something of substance in their annual irritation over the reason for the season? It has become increasingly difficult to find Jesus in the midst of the mad rush to prepare for the 'Holiday Season' and fewer people seem to even care what the festivities are really for. When it comes to the *Christ*-mass element at the heart of all this, misgivings begin to pile up alarmingly.

1. For some, it is doubts that it is simply not true. Snowmen, Santa's little helpers, Good King Wenceslas, tinsel, fir trees, toy grottos, 7 million annual turkey deaths and the claim of a virgin birth are hard to swallow. Even a former Bishop of Durham once voiced the widespread unbelief of many when he said, 'I very much doubt if God would arrange a virgin birth,' apparently assuming that God *would* not, *could* not and *did* not use such an incredible and unscientific means of sending a Saviour. So, if there's no real miracle at the centre, why all this fuss every year?

2. Then there are the effects it has on our spirits. Christmas seems to bring out the worst in us, in spite of our best intentions. There are family rows, hurt and disappointment over being overlooked, and widespread boredom and introspection. Depression, despair and suicide rates rise alarmingly at Christmas, and the Samaritans helpline goes into overdrive.

3. It leaves a massive hole in our bank accounts. Guilt and manipulation are major factors in opening our wallets. Debt spirals out of control. Credit cards exceed all limits. Loan sharks join Herod and go on a 'feeding frenzy'! Unsurprisingly, in spite of our best intentions, most of us exceed our planned budget limits and many take months to pay off their debts.

4. Then there's the anti-climax we feel after it's all over. Who hasn't wondered 'What was that all about?' on Boxing Day, or even earlier? You didn't get what you really wanted. You will be back to work in three days. There's all that mess to clear up, the Christmas tree in the lounge to dispose of and the prospect of snow blocking the roads in the New Year. Why not forget the whole thing?

Yet, in spite of all of these serious reservations about the whole business of what came to be called Christmas, there are a number of reasons why it is entirely appropriate to take time out to celebrate this festival.

1. It is rooted in *fact* and one of the greatest events of all time. An astronaut's first landing on the moon in July 1969 was proudly followed by historic words: 'That's one short step for man, one giant leap for mankind.' But that pales into insignificance compared with God landing on earth in that Bethlehem stable, fully clothed in a human body. This was a totally unprecedented event in world history, a fresh start for the human race. True Christianity is not fiction posing as fact, but faith founded on fact. Jesus is Immanuel – 'God with us' – and therefore God for us, alongside us and to rescue us.

2. Bad people like Herod and his imitators must not be allowed to win. Herod was a 'plant' or 'puppet king' for Rome – ambitious, ruthless, tyrannical and power-crazed. He murdered his wife Mariamne, many Jewish leaders, his own sons, numerous courtiers, countless enemies and most of his critics and rivals. Who would want *him* back? Whatever happened to freedom, truth, openness, tolerance, teachableness, willingness to talk, debate and face up to the truth? The answer is that they have all returned in the one who models kingship perfectly – Jesus.

3. Ban Christmas and we ignore or forfeit all the blessings Christ can bring. Christ's sway and influence continue to transform millions and help to unite nations and all people everywhere – no one is excluded from knowing his healing grace. His birth signalled international mercy now available to all. Jesus Christ elevated the worth of every human life. As an infant he came to redeem infants, as a child to rescue children, as a teen to transform youth, as a young adult to sanctify young manhood and womanhood, as a man to reach the ageing, as a manual worker to dignify the common man, as a king to claim the powerful – all rulers, presidents and kings – so that true peace or God's *shalom* can at last come to all, reconciling humanity to God, to others, to nature and to all things in one reunited order of God's good rule and harmony.

Because of one solitary life, all of our lives can begin again. *Your life can begin again!* So if it would be unwise to ban Christmas, let alone the Christ of Christmas, then why not enjoy Christmas to the full?

Christ came as God in the flesh to die to redeem everything – to turn winter into springtime again, old men into young men again, death into life. This is 'The Year of our Lord', and we would be wise indeed if we came to truly believe it, then live in the amazing truth of it. *Happy Christmas!*

Revd Greg Haslam is Minister of Westminster Chapel in London (www.westminsterchapel.org.uk). He travels widely as a Bible teacher and conference speaker. He has a heart to bring Word and Spirit together through a biblical theology that is on fire. He desires to see the widespread emergence of healthy churches that can become a credible voice to our declining culture. This requires an informed and vigorous depth to their faith, and a dazzlingly different lifestyle in marriage, home, work and Christian community. Greg is married to Ruth and they have three grown-up sons and three grandchildren. He is the author of seven books.

FOUNDATION FOR THE STUDY OF INFANT DEATHS CAROL SERVICE

Graham James

December is a dark month. But late in December we celebrate a small bright light in the birth of Christ. The birth of all children brings hope. It is not simply the promise of a new generation. You see hope in the faces of children: they burn with expectation. Children are strong with promise. That's why grown-ups, often weighed down with too many worries, fall silent in the presence of the new-born.

Christmas is a season of hope. The birth of a child is a protest against those who say that life is meaningless. But the Christmas celebration of the birth at Bethlehem with its carols about joy to the world can trigger stabs of deep sorrow in the hearts of grieving parents and bereaved siblings. Our second daughter, Victoria, died twenty-eight years ago, aged just six months. I can still remember the Christmas which followed as one of the most painful ever to live through. The focus on family at Christmas makes you conscious even years later of the child who isn't there and the adult who never grew. This season has its sorrows as well as its joys for many of us. But a church is a place to bring sorrows as well as joys. It is a place to offer them and not suppress them. It is a place of tenderness and acceptance.

At Christmas we recognise the power of a new-born baby to reshape adult lives. When our first child was born this infant changed our world. Our social life was reshaped. Everything we did was planned to fit in around the smallest member of the family. This small-scale baby had huge power over us. The authority of a child is intriguing to ponder. God chooses this way to reveal himself to us. That's the big surprise at Christmas.

Whenever I watch *University Challenge* on television I get a big thrill out of answering a question which defeats both teams. It doesn't happen very often. That makes the experience even more precious. Not so long ago Jeremy Paxman asked, 'What is beautiful according to a book published by E.F. Schumacher in 1973?' 'Small,' I shouted at the screen in triumph. *Small is Beautiful.* The students hadn't heard of this cult book from my days at university long ago. It shows how quickly cult books go out of fashion.

Schumacher believed the world was beginning to organise itself on too grand a scale. Global corporations and multinational businesses were too big, he claimed. He argued that human beings were made very small scale in a vast universe. We'd lose something of our humanity if we didn't recognise that. That was his theme nearly forty years ago. It is strange that his book has been largely forgotten, since most of what he said has proved to be rather accurate. Some of our economic difficulties have scarcely been helped by the huge scale of our financial institutions. Big isn't so beautiful after all.

We are reminded powerfully of this at Christmas. The birth of Christ is a small-scale event, almost unnoticed in a back street in Bethlehem. The Saviour of the world is introduced to humanity without troubling the mass media of his time. The Christmas story is tiny in human terms.

It is a Christmas tradition that we give toys to our children. A toy is something large brought down to child size. It makes the world more manageable. A train set – that staple gift of fathers to their sons – is a small world in itself. A child's doll is a person in miniature. A toy car is a powerful machine, sometimes beautifully replicated, brought under a small person's control. And so the child experiences the world at a child's level. Play isn't pointless. It is what loved and valued children do. Hungry, uncared-for children don't know how to play.

As Christmas is approaching many of us gather together for a special service because there has been a child in our lives with whom we did not continue playing as long as we wished. We gather also in gratitude for the Foundation for the Study of Infant Deaths and its work, and for the help we were given to live through a parent's worst experience. We come because the child or children whom we loved and lost were deeply precious. When our daughter died there was only one thing which some people said to me that I had to challenge: 'You can have another child to replace her.' We did have another child but no one could replace Victoria. There is no such thing as recycled humanity. And even this distance on, when my wife and I are asked how many children we've got we sometimes feel bad if we don't include Victoria.

If God's wisdom seems like foolishness to human beings, as it says in the Bible, then Christmas illustrates it. It seems absurd that God should become a weak and defenceless infant, living a human life. Yet we know the power of children to change our world. This child called Jesus still fascinates, draws billions of followers, and speaks of the wonder of love. He grew into a man and while Joseph disappears from the story his mother stays with him. She sees her son die on a cross. Mary knew what it was to be a bereaved parent. And if, as Christians have always believed, this child was the Son of God, then God himself knows the experience of a bereaved parent too. And that is the greatest mystery of all.

The Rt Revd Graham James hails from Cornwall, where many members of his family worked in the tin mining industry. He studied History at the University of Lancaster and then did his theological training at Cuddesdon, Oxford. He was ordained in 1975, worked in Welwyn Garden City as a team vicar and then moved to Church House, Westminster where he had responsibility for overseeing the selection procedures for candidates for ordination in the Church of England. In 1987 he was appointed as Chaplain to the Archbishop of Canterbury (Robert Runcie) and continued to work as Archbishop's Chaplain with George Carey during his first two years in office. In 1993 he was consecrated Bishop of St Germans, returning to his native Cornwall. He was enthroned as Bishop of Norwich on 29 January 2000 and is a regular guest on BBC Radio 4's *Thought for the Day*. Graham is married to Julie, a staff nurse, and they have two adult children.

17

THE GIFT
J.John

I love Christmas; it's a time of magical sparkle – I even enjoy the annual tradition of Christmas shopping and present hunting. I see all this as a challenge and adventure – especially when it comes to shopping for my wife Killy.

It hasn't always been easy, though. There has been plenty to learn. When we got engaged, I remember trying to buy Killy a dress for Christmas. I didn't know her size so the woman serving me asked if she was bigger or smaller than her. What could I say … eventually, the shop assistant tried on the dress!

After twenty-nine years of marriage, however, and many hours spent trawling up and down shopping centres, I have developed four criteria when it comes to buying a gift for Killy. It's more of an art form than a precise science but nevertheless, these four things steer me away from the 'panic buy' and towards something more soulful and meaningful. In the process, my four criteria remind me of the gift God has given each of us. What, then, are the four criteria of my gift-buying for my wife Killy at Christmas time?

1. The personal gift

First, I want to make sure my gift for Killy will be *personal* – I want to find something that she can really appreciate. These days, I've stopped buying her what *I* want; after many years of marriage, I now know what *she* likes. After all, it can be very disheartening to receive a present that doesn't have that personal touch.

One of the greatest gifts that we can receive – especially at Christmas time – is the revelation and realisation that God knows each one of us personally and wants us to know him personally, too. When you stop to think about it, it's a mind-blowing thought: God knows us *intimately*. He is not an abstraction or a mystical 'higher power'. Instead, he relates to us on our level. He couldn't possibly have made himself bigger to impress us, so instead he made himself smaller to get alongside us.

Have you ever placed your finger inside the hand of a little baby and felt its grip? If a baby tugs at your finger, it also tugs at your heart. Christmas is the powerful grip of a tiny hand reaching from a bed of straw. It is love, tugging our hearts back to God. And this is the intimately personal nature of Christmas: God gave us his Son for our sake. However, God's gift to us wasn't a one-off that ended when Jesus died for our sins. The Bible tells us that Jesus rose from the dead three days later, and opened the way for us all to live for ever. When he returned to heaven, he sent God's Spirit to live within anyone who would receive him – so that everlasting life could begin now, not just when we get to heaven.

One of Jesus' titles is 'Emmanuel', 'God with us'. For all who choose to make room for him at the inn of their heart, this Jesus has become a gift that could not be more personal.

2. The practical gift

When I buy a gift for Killy, I also want it to be *practical*. Most of us end up receiving at least one or two presents each year that are as much use as a chocolate teapot. Santa might bring us what we deserve; God, however, delivers something we don't deserve. 'For the wages of sin is death,' says the Bible, 'but the gift of God is eternal life in Christ Jesus our Lord' (Romans 6:23). God's *practical* gift to us, then, is forgiveness.

In the run-up to Christmas, we do lots of tidying, preparing and cleaning – sprucing up our homes, our clothes, even our bodies. But Jesus is more concerned with what's on the inside. 'Blessed are the pure in heart,' he said, 'for they will see God' (Matthew 5:8). His *practical* gift is to cleanse our hearts. This changes us from the inside out, transforming our attitudes and actions.

However, we must *want* the gift in order to receive it. We need to pray with the psalmist, who said, 'Create in me a pure heart, O God, and renew a steadfast spirit within me' (Psalm 51:10). Are we hungry for what God has to offer? Jesus was born in Bethlehem, which literally means 'the House of Bread'. Later in his life, he spoke about himself, saying, 'I am the bread of life. Whoever comes to me will never go hungry, and whoever believes in me will never be thirsty' (John 6:35).

Bread satisfies and strengthens, and Jesus came into the world to satisfy and strengthen us all. But this isn't, as we have already seen, a gift to be received passively. It's practical by its very nature. When we receive Jesus, we also receive his Spirit, which helps us to live a brand new kind of life – with love, joy, peace, gentleness, patience, self-control and humility.

3. The permanent gift

So, God's gift is *personal*: he gave us his Son. And God's gift is *practical*, because it helps us to cleanse our lives, satisfying and strengthening us. But when I give a gift to Killy, I also want, if possible, to give something *permanent* – something of lasting value that she will treasure way beyond Christmas Day.

God's gift to us is permanent, not perishable. Listen to those immortal words from John's Gospel: 'For God so loved the world that he gave his one and only Son, that whoever believes in him shall not perish but have eternal life.' God – our heavenly Father – knows that we are all in danger. We're at risk of spending eternity separated from him. That's why God sent Jesus – it was to give us the opportunity to go to heaven. 'Truly I tell you,' he said, 'whoever hears my word and believes him who sent me has eternal life and will not be judged but has crossed over from death to life' (John 5:24). Life without Christ is a hopeless end, but life with Christ is an endless hope.

4. The purchased gift

So, God's gift is *personal, practical* and *permanent.* But when I find a gift for Killy, I also like to *purchase* it before walking out of the shop!

God's gift to us was, likewise, purchased. It didn't come for free – in fact, it came at a huge cost and we should not cheapen it by discarding it lightly. God gave us his only Son. We couldn't save ourselves, so Jesus came to rescue us. If we try to save ourselves, God can't save us. Jesus rescued us by purchasing forgiveness when he died on the cross. The Bible says, 'He is the atoning sacrifice for our sins' (1 John 2:2).

This is the startling truth of the gospel – Jesus Christ has purchased our redemption. We now have to receive that gift for ourselves, acknowledging that there's nothing more we can do to attain God's forgiveness than accepting it through his Son Jesus. We are saved by having faith in Jesus to rescue us – not by doing good works. God spent everything he had on us. And the gift is one that we shouldn't want to exchange for anything else.

God doesn't force himself upon anyone, however. He offers his gift, but he won't make you take it. He's already reached out to us through the life and death of his Son. It's up to us to make the next move.

Revd Canon J.John lives in Chorleywood, Hertfordshire in England. He is married to Killy and they have three sons, Michael, Simeon and Benjamin. J.John is a speaker with an appeal that transcends gender, age, race, culture and occupation. To date, he has completed thousands of speaking engagements in sixty-nine countries on six continents. J.John has also authored several titles. For more information, see www.philotrust.com (www.twitter.com/Canonjjohn).

MORE THAN A CHRISTMAS CAROL
J.John

You may feel that you are familiar with the story of Christmas, that you don't need to take another look. But we can all get so used to things that we ignore the detail. We think we know what it's all about, but do we really?

Take Charles Dickens' *A Christmas Carol*. It has been adapted into over 200 films and is such a powerful story that it's credited with helping to define our contemporary understanding of Christmas. But a fresh look reminds us that it's far more than a feel-good festive tale – the story of Ebenezer Scrooge and his tormenting spirits helps us to consider what is of eternal value, here in the twenty-first century. Ebenezer Scrooge is the mean and intimidating character, who lives to make money and very little else. He certainly has no use for religion or sentimentality.

One Christmas Eve, however, Scrooge receives a terrifying wake-up call. The spirit of his business partner, Jacob Marley, comes to visit, bound and wrapped in terrible chains. Marley has been condemned to roam the face of the earth, tormented by the things he neglected to value in life. He is desperate to help his old colleague avoid the same fate. Marley tells Scrooge to wait for three more spirits of Christmas to appear and, on the stroke of one o'clock, the Spirit of Christmas Past arrives. He takes Scrooge on a trip down memory lane, to Scrooge's own childhood. He sees old, familiar faces playing happily but as the spirit takes him into a schoolroom, they see a lonely little boy sitting by the fire, his only companion the book he is reading.

Scrooge remembers his loneliness, and how he longed for the presence and warmth of friends. He then sees all the people who tried to reach out to stop his slide into self-absorption, and his former fiancée, Belle, who came a poor second to Scrooge's passion for wealth. Through Scrooge's ordeal, Dickens explores the love of money compared with the value of relationships. We can fall into a similar trap, seeing money as the answer to our problems. And if we start to feel guilty, we excuse ourselves with the thought that we want our children to have the things we missed out on.

Jacob Marley's ghostly visit is not just a wake-up call for Scrooge – we should make sure *we* haven't lost out on the things that money can't buy. It's as if society has caught a disease called 'affluenza': the symptoms include always wanting more, despite what we already have. Consistently, we choose our career over family and we seem unwilling to settle for less than the best of everything.

If Scrooge is shaken by the visit of the first spirit, the second is no less disturbing. The Spirit of Christmas Present takes Scrooge on a tour of the people he now knows. He finds himself in the home of his clerk, Bob Cratchit, where he feels the warmth of a large, friendly family making the best of what little they can afford on the tiny salary he pays. He experiences their anxiety about Tiny Tim, their sick youngest child. Scrooge is shown the effects of his selfish nature but also that others have not entirely given up on him. As they sit down to their feeble Christmas dinner, Bob Cratchit nevertheless toasts his boss.

The spirit then shows Scrooge the reality of life on the streets, and the determination of the families living there to stay out of the prisons and workhouses. Scrooge has always believed that the poor 'should go to the institutions provided – if they should rather die, let them die and reduce the surplus population'. But his heart is softening …

Then comes the Spirit of Christmas Future. Scrooge sees the Cratchit family again, worn down and now without Tiny Tim, who has died for lack of proper medical care. Then the spirit takes Scrooge to the house of a man who has died in his sleep. A maid and a cleaner are dividing up his belongings and others are discussing whether it's even necessary to hold a funeral service, since no one would come. 'Who is this man?' asks Scrooge. The spirit points to a gravestone bearing the name 'Ebenezer Scrooge'.

This is when he understands that it's now or never: is it possible to mend his ways and alter his destiny? As Christmas morning dawns, Scrooge realises that he *has* been given a reprieve. He has another opportunity to be more human.

Many of us will recognise the struggles of Ebenezer Scrooge. We have been hurt as we grew up or have passed up the offer of friendship or kindness, fearing rejection. Scrooge lived in a prison of his own making, the doors sealed with a bitterness he wouldn't let go. The good news is that we can learn from the past, changing now so that we can create a better future. God knows us better than we know ourselves, and loves us enough to help us to change.

If you are still making a Christmas list, these timeless gifts won't cost you anything, except perhaps a little pride: you could mend a quarrel; release a grudge; lessen your demands on others; apologise; forgive someone who has treated you wrongly; find a forgotten friend; write an overdue thank-you note; point out something you appreciate about someone you live with or work with; dismiss suspicion; tell someone you love them; or give something away. You cannot do a kindness too soon, because you never know how soon it will be too late.

It takes a conscious, personal decision to become a follower of Jesus, acknowledging that we all need him – to forgive us for what we have done wrong, and to guide us into *real* life, the life he promised to give us 'to the full'. Jesus isn't just another pick-and-mix lifestyle guru. If we choose to follow him, then we also have to count the cost – of dedication, commitment, perseverance, selfless love and generosity. But the reward – a dynamic, living relationship with the dynamic, living God – is surely worth it.

Dickens sent a message to us in the form of an amazing story. God sends his message in the form of his Son, Jesus Christ.

Revd Canon J.John lives in Chorleywood, Hertfordshire in England. He is married to Killy and they have three sons, Michael, Simeon and Benjamin. J.John is a speaker with an appeal that transcends gender, age, race, culture and occupation. To date, he has completed thousands of speaking engagements in sixty-nine countries on six continents. J.John has also authored several titles. For more information, see www.philotrust.com (www. twitter.com/Canonjjohn).

THE FIRST GREAT AWAKENING
R. T. Kendall

The first great awakening described in the New Testament is when the Magi came from the east to Jerusalem asking, 'Where is the one who has been born king of the Jews? We saw his star when it rose and have come to worship him' (Matthew 2:1–2). The result was that King Herod was shaken rigid and all Jerusalem with him (v.3). And yet, sadly, there is no evidence that any of the people – and certainly not the king – were converted as a consequence of the Magi's question. While not all awakenings – or times of revival – are the same, the account described in Matthew 2 shows a definite pattern.

First, an ***unexpected people*** tend to appear when God works powerfully. The prophet Zechariah forecast that 'those who are far away will come and help to build the temple of the LORD' (Zechariah 6:15). The Magi were undoubtedly seekers of God motivated by a sincere desire to find the Christ child. They were not Jews but this was a hint that the salvation brought by Jesus Christ would be for 'all the people' (Luke 2:10). These men were certainly an unexpected people – a mysterious people from the east. They probably came from Persia (today's Iran), about 1,000 miles away. Riding on camels it took many months for them to arrive at Jerusalem.

Second, an ***unusual providence*** often occasions a great awakening. 'We saw his star,' they announced to the people of Jerusalem. They were in the east, and the star which they followed was in the west. For many months they had been following this star. Only God could have been behind this. There is no verse in the Old Testament alerting the leaders of the Jews to watch out for a star; it was an unusual providence that coincided with Jesus' birth. But so, too, with many awakenings – things happen that nobody anticipated.

In Hebrews 11 we have the 'faith' chapter of the Bible. All these men and women did extraordinary things by *faith.* They also had in common that not one of them did what had been done before. They all had to do what was *unprecedented:* Enoch walked with God and was translated; Noah walked with God and was commanded to build an ark; Abraham walked with God and did not even know where he was going (Hebrews 11:8). When God does unusual things it frequently requires us to do what has not been done before. For the Magi it was the providence of the star that led them to Jesus.

Third, a **universal provocation** followed. 'When King Herod heard this he was *disturbed*, and all Jerusalem with him' (Matthew 2:3). Not just King Herod but '*all* Jerusalem with him' reacted the same way. The whole city was shaken – merely by the question put by the Magi! This is what happens when a genuine awakening takes place. It became a common pattern in the New Testament. People were filled with 'awe' or 'fear' when Jesus performed miracles (Luke 5:26), it was part of the fall-out of the Day of Pentecost – 'everyone was filled with awe' (Acts 2:43); and fear was what people felt when Ananias and Sapphira lied to the Holy Spirit (Acts 5:11).

There is not much fear of God in the church today; people are attracted by what gives them a good feeling. But don't expect that a great awakening will be warmly welcomed and appreciated. Take, for example, Jesus casting out demons. It was a needed ministry but it scared people – however impressed and amazed they were that demon-possessed people were delivered, the community still pleaded with Jesus to leave their region (Matthew 8:34).

Fourth, an **unlikely pursuit** followed the provocation – people reading the Bible! Herod called for the people's chief priests and teachers of the Law to ask where the Messiah was to be born. The religious leaders knew the answer, for the prophet Micah had written: 'But you, Bethlehem Ephrathah, though you are small among the clans of Judah, out of you will come for me one who will be ruler over Israel' (Micah 5:2).

There is nothing like a move of the Holy Spirit to get people to turn to the word of God. This is what was happening – the Magi were being led by the Holy Spirit, but they too still had a lot to learn. They thought that the star leading them to Jerusalem could only mean that Christ would be born in Jerusalem. No, it would be Bethlehem. But never had there been such a sudden turning to Scripture – all because of the Magi.

Fifth, sadly, a great awakening often leads to **unwarranted professions.** King Herod feigned an interest in spiritual things and sent the Magi to Bethlehem saying, 'As soon as you find him, report to me, so that I too may go and worship him' (Matthew 2:8). They had no reason to doubt the sincerity of King Herod at the time but King Herod was not interested in worshipping the Christ-child. He wanted to destroy the child, and he later 'gave orders to kill all the boys in Bethlehem and its vicinity who were two years old and under, in accordance with the time he had learned from the Magi' (Matthew 2:16).

A general awakening creates a religious spirit that may or may not lead to conversion. The 'bandwagon' effect can occur when there is a widespread interest in the things of God. People may seek the Lord because of financial reverse, marital problems, illness, loneliness or a sudden crisis. God *can* use these things to get our attention and bring us to himself but a sudden religious interest is in itself no proof of conversion. How do you know you have been genuinely converted by the Holy Spirit? When you have abandoned all hope in good works and have transferred your trust to Jesus Christ alone. Only the Holy Spirit brings a person to faith like that.

Finally, there is an **unmistakable preservation** inherent in a sovereign work of God. God preserved the Magi, despite King Herod. They went on their way and the star led them directly to where the child was. God preserved them. They came to a house – perhaps two years after Jesus' birth – and saw the child, bowed down and worshipped him (Matthew 2:11). Those who seek the Lord with all their hearts find him – and are kept by him. He who has begun a good work in us will 'carry it on to completion until the day of Christ Jesus' (Philippians 1:6).

Perhaps the saddest thing about the first great awakening is that only the Magi cared to go to Bethlehem to see where this child was. It is therefore not surprising that the Jews rejected their Messiah some thirty-three years later. They simply did not want God to intrude into their lives. Bethlehem was only six miles away! They could not be bothered to find the very person Israel claimed to wait for! The Magi were focused on one thing – getting to Jesus. That is what a great awakening is all about.

Dr R.T. Kendall was born in Ashland, Kentucky on 13 July 1935. He was the minister of Westminster Chapel for twenty-five years. He now writes books and travels internationally, holding Bible conferences. He has two children (TR and Melissa) and one grandson. He and his wife Louise live in Nashville, Tennessee, USA. For more information, see www.RTKendallministries.com.

PREFER ONE ANOTHER: SELFLESSNESS
David McDougall

There is a story about how, years ago, there was an old man who used to walk the streets of the seaport town in France and whom they called 'The Miser of Marseilles'. He was an object of derision throughout the whole city and even throughout the south of France, for everybody seemed to know him. Apparently he loved nothing and had no other object than to hoard every bit of money he got hold of; for what purpose, no one knew. He was hated whenever he appeared on the streets. When he died, he was so despised that only a single person attended his funeral. Then his will was read, and these were its strange terms:

> *From my infancy I noticed that the poor people of Marseilles had great difficulty in getting water. I noticed that water, the gift of God, was very dear and difficult to obtain. And when they could get that water, it was not as pure and clean as God intended it to be. Therefore, I vowed before God that I would live but for one purpose, for one end. I would save money, money, money; that I might give it to the city on one condition: that an aqueduct be built to bring fresh, pure water from yonder lake in the hills to Marseilles. That I now make possible by leaving all my hoarded wealth to this city. This is my last will and testament.*

Travellers in Marseilles today hear the poor people say as they drink the pure, sweet water from the lake in the hills, 'Ah, when the miser died, we misunderstood him, but he did it all for us! We called him the miser of Marseilles, but he was more than that; he was the saviour of Marseilles.'

What would happen if we were to really grasp the meaning of this story? That the secret of how to get the most out of life is to *give* the most to life. What a different world it would be if we were the first to give the present rather than selfishly waiting for the gifts to be lavished on us.

Joseph – an example of selflessness

Joseph was chosen by God to be the earthly father of Jesus (Matthew 1:18–25). Would he be up to the role? He must have felt as if a ton of bricks had been dropped on him when he got word that Mary was expecting a child. But Joseph was a godly man (Matthew 1:19a), a considered man in his actions (Matthew 1:19b–20a) and not willing to make Mary a public example. He was thinking about divorcing her quietly but while he was thinking about this an angel came. To expose her to public shame – what would that have meant at that time in that culture? Adultery has always been considered a very serious crime. In Egypt, it was punished by cutting off the nose of the adulteress; in Persia, the nose and ears were cut off; in Judea, the punishment was death by stoning. This punishment was also inflicted where the person was not married but betrothed. In this case, therefore, the regular punishment would have been death.

Joseph was **a mild and tender man**. He was not willing to complain about Mary to the magistrate and expose her to death. He decided to avoid the shame and to divorce her quietly.

There is so much we can learn from Joseph this Christmas:

- *He controlled his emotions*
  It would have been so easy for Joseph to let his emotions get to him. He could very easily have exploded. This happens all the time, even to people who claim they love the Lord. He could easily have thrown a temper tantrum and disqualified himself for the Lord's service.

- *He controlled his judgement*
  Now let's be honest – what do you think Joseph first thought when Mary told him she was pregnant? He must have been initially very critical in his thinking. However, he controlled his judgement and handled himself well.

- *He controlled his impatience*
  'But after he had considered this …' (Matthew 1:20). Here
  we can see that, like Mary, he thought deeply and
  therefore responded wisely to the call of God on his life.

Joseph was *a genuine man* (Matthew 1:20b–23). He knew the word
of God – 'Therefore the Lord himself will give you a sign: the virgin
will conceive and give birth to a son, and will call him Immanuel'
(Isaiah 7:14).

Joseph believed the word of God and Joseph lived the word of God.
He was *an obedient man.* Everything in Joseph's life was turned in
a new direction. His disappointment was transformed into understanding and joy, and instead of divorcing Mary, he married her.
Then, instead of consummating the marriage, he exercised great
restraint. And all because an angel came to him with the glorious
gospel of salvation in the Lord Jesus Christ.

All the changes that took place in Joseph's life took place because
he accepted by faith the truth of God about his Son, Jesus Christ.

Joseph was *a sacrificial man* (Matthew 1:25). He sacrificed his
pride, his dreams, and his rights as a husband. Joseph is utterly
selfless and presents Jesus to the world as the most wonderful
present – a totally selfless act.

- Jesus is the most selfless person who ever existed.

- Jesus came to find you.

- Jesus lived so that you might live.

- Jesus died so that you might not fear death.

- Jesus died so that in his death all our wrong choices can
  be forgiven.

- Jesus rose again from the dead so that you might have
  everlasting life in him.

- Jesus even sent his very Spirit – to enable you to live life
  to the very fullest.

- Jesus was all about others.

- Jesus was utterly selfless in every way.

This Christmas, let's live like Jesus with the total aim of:

- Preferring others.
- Putting others first.
- Finding ways to really bless the socks off other people.
- Surprising people by generosity and kindness and hospitality.

All in the spirit of Christian love.

Revd David McDougall is the Vicar of St Saviour's, Sunbury (see www.st-saviours-sunbury.org.uk) and Area Dean of Spelthorne in the Kensington Episcopal Area of London. David is married to Kim and they have three grown-up children. David planted St Saviour's Anglican Church, which has grown from 50 to 350 in nine years. He travels widely, believing that mission needs to be at 'home and away'.

21

EMMANUEL: GOD IS WITH US
Simon McIntyre

'God is with us' is the heart of the Christmas message – because it is the meaning of the name, Jesus. The Christmas event is a person and he has a name – Jesus. Anything less is less. But Christmas has been turned into almost anything but 'God with us'. In the West it has taken on the look of family, food, presents, holidays, carols – all great things, things we all enjoy and celebrate, but *not* the main thing. Jesus should have centre stage. He doesn't share the limelight with lesser actors, insipid scripts and bit parts.

In the Christian world the theme of Christmas often ends up being 'peace' or 'neighbourly kindness' or 'charitable acts' to others. Again, these are all good things, and not to be minimised, but they should not be emphasised at the cost of the main thing – the incarnation of God in Jesus.

'God is with us' is the most important thing you can know about how God is in relation to me, to you and to others, but often it is the least believed and accepted thing about God. Why is this?

We shy away from God because guilt plagues humanity and has done so since the very beginning (Genesis 3:1–11). We misread God's presence as one of fear and judgement and this is precisely what religion has tried to appease. All sorts of saints and sacraments have been placed between us and God. Although the purpose of these things may be to create a mediated pathway to God they end up compounding the distance – a distance Christ has dealt a death blow to. We too easily re-sew the curtain of the temple that was split in two at the death of Jesus, signifying that the way was now open.

And we find it hard to accept that 'God is with us' because we are internally conflicted and hardly 'for' ourselves some days. Adam's expulsion from the garden was the beginning of our estrangement from God. We don't feel right and therefore we misinterpret God's action towards us as that of a distant and angry deity – which is partly the reason he got 'up close and personal' in Jesus.

Christmas changes everything – for ever. God has declared in Christ that he is 'with' and 'for us' – not 'away from' or 'against' us. This is Good News. His love is larger than our sin, fears or guilt. It eclipses them and blots them out. His answer is that he is for you, with you, near you – loving you. This is nowhere better summed up than in the majestic words of Paul in Romans 8:31–39: 'If God is for us, who can be against us?' With someone like God being for you there is no other circumstance or power that matches up. God's 'for-ness' overcomes any other 'against-ness'.

If God didn't spare the gift of his Son, and there is nothing else that can better that, then everything else is ours as well. He won't withhold anything when he has already given the very best – himself.

God gave us 'right standing' (in judicial terminology), and Christ died and was raised for us. Nothing we did or can do gives us right standing, therefore nothing we did or can do will undo his grace towards us. This is hardly cause for lazy living – it is cause for praise and gratefulness and right living. Satan is the accuser – it is his name and strategy to defeat God's people. But Paul asks who can accuse us or condemn us (Romans 8:33–34).

Paul then asks if troubles can separate us from God's love. It is a rhetorical question, as nothing can separate us; on the contrary, 'despite all these things, overwhelming victory is ours through Christ, who loved us' (Romans 8:37, *New Living Translation*).

Then Paul finishes by saying that *nothing* can separate us from God's love, and he names all the big ones – death, life, angels, powers, demons – you name it, it isn't sufficient to separate us. We read troubles as a sign of disfavour and even rejection by God, which is why it is so important to understand that 'God is with us'.

The story of Elisha in 2 Kings 6:8–18 is a graphic example of 'God is with us'. Fear prevents us from seeing the protection and greatness of God and faith opens our eyes to see. Lord, open our eyes! Then we begin to see that God is close and give testimony to this in a variety of ways:

- God is for me and with me – on my side, by my side.

- God is for me – he is not against us, opposed to us or angry with us.

- God is with me – I'm not alone, I'm never alone.

- God is for me – everything will work out according to his plan. Life isn't a series of meaningless occasions or mistakes.

- God is with me – circumstances can and will change but God will fortify me in the middle of them.

- God is for me – everyone else may not be and maybe there are reasons, but nevertheless God is for me. I might not be 'for' me but he is 'for' me.

- God is with me – he isn't far away, he made the journey to my world. This is precisely the story of Christmas, once we get past the trees, gifts, turkey, stuffing and pudding.

'Emmanuel' – this is Christmas, and cause for the celebrations we enjoy.

Pastor Simon McIntyre, along with his wife Valerie, is currently the Pastor of C3 London, Overseer of C3 Churches in Europe/UK and a Director of C3 Global (see www.c3london.com). His church background is rich and varied and he identifies his gift as 'doing what needs to be done'. Simon is a great fan of and believer in the church. His style of communication has been described by some as refreshing, by others as always relevant and by some as 'alarming'. When time allows he flies an aerobatic plane, writes books and sits on a beach – not all at the same time.

MERRY CHRISTMAS, EVERYONE!
Keith 'Mitch' Mitchell

Who is excited about Christmas? Who has made a list for Santa? And tell me … who has been good enough to get a few presents?

Christmas Day is such an exciting one, with lots happening and very often in all the excitement it's easy to forget what really matters. There is a little verse in the Bible that says, 'Don't let the excitement of youth cause you to forget your Creator' (Ecclesiastes 12:1, *New Living Translation*).

On Christmas Day, in all the excitement and fun, do not forget about God. Do not forget the baby Jesus in the manger. I want you to have a cracking Christmas, but I want you to remember Jesus and his love for each one of you. The best Christmas present isn't wrapped in paper. The best present isn't even wrapped in foil and tinsel. The best present is wrapped in swaddling clothes and lying in a manger. In the excitement of being young, in the excitement of Christmas, do not forget God.

What is Christmas really all about? I'll give you a clue: it's in the name, Christmas, a celebration of Christ. We celebrate the fact that the King of Heaven willingly stepped from his throne, removed his crown and royal robe and descended into our world. He was birthed into a cold night among sheep, cows, donkeys and bugs … C.S. Lewis describes it like this: God has landed on this enemy-occupied world in human form. He breathes our air, cries for his milk and depends on the very people he created to warm him and love him. Jesus, the all-time, undisputed champion of love arrives for the main event weighing in at 7lb, 7oz with hiccups!

2 Corinthians 8:9 is one of my favourite verses and in many ways sums up Christmas. Paul wrote, 'For you know the grace of our Lord Jesus Christ, that though he was rich, yet for your sake he became poor, so that you through his poverty might become rich.' Jesus would give up the riches of heaven to lie in an animal feeder. His mother, a little teenage girl, had no idea what to do with a Saviour who is now crying for milk while his surrogate father Joseph watches on in wonder ... what will become of this child?

Come and look into the manger. That is your King in there, your Saviour, your hope. This is a *very* special moment: but what will become of this child? The manger has a *dark shadow*. The shadow lets us see that there is something very significant about the baby who will lie in the manger and what his future holds. One picture can tell a whole story – a dark shadow of destiny cast over a manger shows the significance of the baby.

An angel helps us to understand more, declaring 'A Saviour has been born' and the dark shadow cast across the manger would be significant for this Saviour. The baby sleeping in a manger would one day hang on a cross. Those hands that playfully reached out to his mother would one day be pierced by nails. One picture can tell a whole story and the Christmas manger is incomplete without the cross.

Now, step away from the manger and go outside to see how this child will grow.

For the next thirty-three years or so God will live on planet Earth, as a boy called Jesus Bar Joseph. He will walk to school, play games with his friends and avoid the vices of Nazareth, a hotbed of terrorist activity even to this day ... At thirteen years of age Jesus will stand before the congregation of the temple during bar-mitzvah and declare, 'Today I am a man.' God declares, 'Today I am a man.' In the Bible there are seven 'I am' sayings but this one does it for me ...

As a teenager he will be about his father's business – that of his surrogate father Joseph, in learning the trade of a carpenter. Among other things he would hone his skills ... soon, making a yoke would become easy. And he will be about the business of his heavenly Father, in studying the Scriptures and praying. No doubt the Rabbi schoolteachers would have been impressed with his passion and knowledge during RE.

As a man he will be known to many as a faith healer, preacher, prophet and Rabbi but to others as a man of sorrows acquainted with grief. Emmanuel, 'God with us', is now beaten, nailed and bleeding – covered in spit and naked, his lips are cracked and swollen. For six hours, God is on a cross … and that's your sin he is feeling, your punishment, your death. That's how much he loves you.

Let's go back inside shall we? Back to the manger. We had to go outside and see what he will become in order to understand what is happening inside.

This was a birth, on an ordinary night, for ordinary people: people like you and me. The shepherds were ordinary geezers, if anything they were rough diamonds, vagabonds and thieves but God includes them in the story … why? And why would Jesus later call tax collectors and fishermen to follow him? Would it not have been better to have a few governors, scribes and historians there to verify the account? But Jesus didn't come for a particular people group. He didn't come for the religious scholars, the righteous, the educated, the rich or the talented. No, he came as a gift for everyone, including you and me. It doesn't matter what your situation or predicament … Jesus has answers. That's what makes this gift so special; it is for everyone.

That first Christmas, ordinary people encounter the extraordinary King. The supernatural meets the natural, the Creator meets the created, the King of heaven meets peasants on the hillside, the Immortal meets the mortal. No wonder the apostle Paul calls him the 'indescribable gift' (2 Corinthians 9:15).

And it gets better … 2,000 years later Jesus is still doing the same and touching the lives of ordinary people. Maybe he will do it today for you? By remembering Jesus, understanding his mission, recognising your need for him and receiving this free gift you can enter into a real living relationship with Jesus. Today you can invite Jesus to take up residence in your heart. The innkeeper had no room for him … but what about you?

This supernatural, extraordinary unspeakable gift is offered to you today. It is a gift not for the righteous but the unrighteous, it is for weak-kneed, struggling people like you and me.

Keith 'Mitch' Mitchell is co-founder of Crown Jesus Ministries in Ireland (see www.crownjesus.org). Having served sixteen years as a fire-fighter, he is now in full-time ministry as a speaker. His energy, wit, honesty and passion allow him to communicate in a relevant way to today's society. He is married to Amanda and they have two children.

THE BIRTH OF JESUS
Nigel Mumford

The day is here, dear friends, Merry Christmas. Wouldn't it be wonderful if the House of the Lord was as full every Sunday as it is on Christmas Day? I am going to keep praying that one day it will be. It is so good to see so many people as we celebrate the birth of our Lord Jesus Christ. Christmas can be an emotionally charged celebration as the commercial stress piles on us and as we search for that perfect gift. As we load up our refrigerators and pantries with the fare of the season. The smells, the sights, the lights, all the senses filled, triggering memories of Christmas past. Wonderful childhood memories of peeking through the music room glass door at the tree and the gifts around the tree. We were allowed to take a peek and then went to church. The gifts were opened after church with such a crescendo of expectation. As an adult now, watching the children open gifts is such a joy.

As I wrote this sermon I thought, What on earth would have happened if Mary said 'No' to the angel? Would the angel have flown off to find someone else? Did God have a plan B? What would have happened if Joseph had said no? They both said yes to God. A life-changing decision. A world-changing decision. Saying yes to God when we are prompted is indeed a life-changing decision. Luke writes that Joseph went to register with Mary, who was pledged to be married to him and was expecting a child. It is quite clear that they were not married at this point in the journey. The innkeeper assumed they were married. Anything could have gone wrong but God was in charge. Jesus was born and placed in a manger – the Son of God in a manger.

I have to confess that I can be a bit of a dreamer and can quite easily see in my mind's eye what was going on. Having been to Bethlehem it is very easy to 'see' the picture. I put myself there as a shepherd. Totally freaked out, 'terrified' at seeing an angel, and then hearing the proclamation, 'Today in the town of David a Saviour has been born to you; he is the Messiah, the Lord' (Luke 2:11). Then, just to make sure we got the message, a whole host of heavenly beings appeared. They were praising God, saying, 'Glory to God in the highest heaven, and on earth peace to those on whom his favour rests' (Luke 2:14). OK, OK we got the message! Wow …

Then wandering on my way to the stable as fast as my legs could go. My heart pounding, not even able to speak to my fellow shepherds … On this day the Christ-child Jesus is born. The Son of man, right here. There we found a baby wrapped in cloths and lying in a manger.

Can you imagine it? I can. I can smell the hay; I can see everything … God has given us a gift of imagination; it is good to use it. Dream a little!

The shepherds then ran off to tell everyone … what excitement in Bethlehem that night. Can you imagine the locals? 'Hey, Jesus the Son of God has been born down the road, you must come and see!' Would you leave your pint and run down the road? I think I would take my pint and sprint down the road … Can you imagine the conversations in the pub the next day?

There was no room for God in the inn. Is that an analogy and lifelong message from God himself? Is there room for God in *your* house? If a pregnant couple knocked on your door what would you do? Call 999 on your mobile?

A life-changing moment? No, a world-changing moment in the history of humanity. A moment when God set his foot on the world again, giving us hope, peace, love, healing grace, eternal life and so much more.

'The shepherds returned, glorifying and praising God for all the things they had heard and seen, which were just as they had been told' (Luke 2:20). How did they just go back to work? I am sure the sheep had been somewhat spooked by the heavenly hosts buzzing around. Perhaps they had to spend the next few hours looking for their sheep. I see them stumbling around laughing, 'Hey, I got one of yours over here …' 'What joy. We have seen Jesus …'

Perhaps you are hurting, perhaps you need healing, perhaps you need joy back in your heart? Come with me, walk with me. As a shepherd, let me walk with you towards the light in the stable. I am standing beside you, walking with you. No words are needed. There is great light, almost daylight from the star. We can see it all. As we approach, Joseph ushers us in. Mary looks up and smiles at us. She lets us look into the manger. There he is, Jesus the Son of God, looking at you, smiling at you, beaming. He is so very pleased to see you. Mary is thanking you for coming to see them.

Mary then picks up the Christ-child and holds him for a while as we just stand in awe. She then moves closer to you, smiles at you, and then hands over the Son of God for you to hold. You take him in your arms. You hold Jesus; you look deeply into his eyes. He grabs your little finger and holds tightly on to it. You know the peace of God flowing in your very bloodstream. No words are needed. His eyes penetrate right into your soul. Jesus smiles even more as your heart melts and you know. Time stands still. Breathe in that love. Breathe in the love of Jesus. Allow the Christ-child to heal your wounds. Jesus came to set the captives free and to heal us. God has let you into his master plan. Receive that love and receive that healing.

Revd Nigel W.D. Mumford is an Episcopal priest and the director of the healing ministry at Christ the King, Spiritual Life Center, Greenwich New York, USA. Fr Mumford was born and educated in England and served for six and a half years in Her Majesty's Royal Marine Commandos. His last two years as a Marine were spent as a drill instructor at the Commando Training School. His conviction to pray for healing came in 1989 when his sister, Julie Sheldon, a ballet dancer with the Royal Ballet in London, was healed by God through the late Canon Jim Glennon. Fr Mumford has three published books: *Hand to Hand: From Combat to Healing* (Church Publishing Inc), *The Forgotten Touch* (Seabury Press) and *After the Trauma the Battle Begins: Post Trauma Healing* (Troy Bookmakers). Nigel lives with his wife Lynn near Saratoga Springs, New York, USA.

WHAT IF THERE WAS NO CHRISTMAS?
Rich Nathan

I read in the paper the other day that there are 2.6 billion Christmas cards mailed during the Christmas season. Some businesses take in over half of their annual retail business in the month preceding Christmas. Why, if there was no Christmas, lots of people would be out of work. The whole country could slide into recession.

But is the effect of Christmas simply financial? What if there was no Christmas? You know, Christmas is the holiday celebrating the birth of Jesus. It is not just about gift giving and trees. It is not just about family gatherings and chestnuts roasting on an open fire. Christmas is not just about mistletoe and sleigh bells ringing in the snow. Christmas is a holiday celebrating the birth of Jesus.

And so when we ask the question: what if there was no Christmas, I am really asking – what if Jesus had never been born? How big a hole would be left in this world? What is the impact of the birth of Christ on the way that this world now functions?

Someone once said that you can tell the size of a boat by the size of the wake it leaves behind. An ocean liner will create an enormous tidal wave in its wake, a small sailboat hardly leaves a ripple. The same thing can be true of a man or a woman. The world is changed for ever because of the impact of that one life. And when some people are gone there is almost nothing left that says that they passed this way.

What did Christ leave behind in the wake of his life? It is interesting to consider what Jesus *didn't* leave behind. We have no photo of Christ.

We have no contemporaneous painting or sculpture. We don't know what Jesus looked like. We don't know if he was tall or short or fat or thin. We have no furniture from his carpenter's shop. You can't visit Jesus' boyhood home the way you can visit the palaces of the kings and queens of England, Russia or Holland. We don't have any memoirs written by Christ in his own pen, not a single word written in his own hand.

So in some ways, his life was like a sailboat; it left nothing behind. Jesus came into the world virtually unnoticed, born in some frontier village on the eastern edge of the Roman Empire. Apart from his teenage unwed mother and her soon-to-be-husband, Joseph, the only living creatures to witness the birth of Christ were some cattle.

And yet, the wake that was created by the life of this man Jesus, the size of the wake, was enough to cover the world with a tidal wave several miles high. The hole left in the world, if there was no Christmas, would be the size of a continent. C.S. Lewis said that without the birth of Christ, it would always be winter, but never Christmas.

What if there was no Christmas? It was a dangerous thing to be conceived in the ancient world. Indeed, life outside of the Christian world has often been exceedingly cheap. But then Jesus was born. And because Jesus was born, his followers took on Jesus' view of life. To Jesus every life was precious – the life of the unborn, the life of children, the life of the elderly, the life of the infirm. To Jesus, life was a sacred gift. And this whole view of life as a sacred gift is now foundational to the whole way our society is structured.

But not only in Jesus do we have a view of the sacredness of life, but Christ's life was characterised by a passionate care for the least in society – the sick, the elderly, the widow, the orphans, the leper, the prostitute. In the wake of Christ coming, we see a concern for the weakest in our society. In a world without Christ, it is always the strong who win. But because of Jesus, the strong, the powerful, the wealthy are often willing to take a back seat to promote the interests of the weak, the least, the last and the lost. What a difference the life of Christ has made. What an extraordinary wake he has left. The strong taking care of the weak.

What did Jesus leave behind? No house, no clothes, no pictures. What was left in the wake of the life of Jesus was the revelation of God. If there was no Christmas – if God did not come into the world, if God had not taken on human flesh and allowed himself to be born in a stable – then we would not know him. We would not know God and we would have no possibility of being changed or being saved. By coming into the world and taking on human flesh, God showed us what he was like. And what is God like as he came to us in the personhood of Jesus? The God revealed by Jesus is one whom you can approach, whom you can get near to, whom you can be intimate with.

In your most honest moments, when you are entirely alone, the biggest secret you have, whether you have been a great success or a great failure, is that you need God. Do you know what Jesus left in his wake? He left God. Not just social betterment. Not just a better way to live. Jesus left God.

Pastor Dr Rich Nathan has been serving as the first senior pastor of the Vineyard, Columbus, since 1987 (see www.vineyardcolumbus.org). Prior to pastoring, Rich taught Business Law at Ohio State University for five years. He has served on the National Board for Vineyard: A Community of Churches for over two decades and is currently serving as the Large Church Task Force Leader for the Vineyard. He is a popular national and international conference speaker. Rich is the author of *Who is My Enemy? Welcoming People the Church Rejects* (Zondervan, 2002) and co-authored *Empowered Evangelicals* (Ampelon, Revised 2009) with Ken Wilson. Rich was born and raised in New York City. He and his wife Marlene have been married for thirty-five years. They have two children and seven grandchildren.

MEET THE REAL JESUS
Haydn Nelson

Have you ever inadvertently confused someone with someone else? We can all laugh at this type of common mix-up because, relatively speaking, it doesn't have big implications for us. But what if it were different? What if meeting or not meeting a particular person had huge implications for us? What if the identity of a person was so profoundly significant that, if we *didn't* realise who they were, we'd regret it for ever – but if we *did* realise who they were, we'd be for ever grateful? I don't think any of us would want to miss someone like that, would we?

In the Bible we hear a lot about Jesus – both what he said and what he did. And, considering the things Jesus said and the things Jesus did, this is not someone we'd want to miss. In fact, the message of Christianity is that knowing or not knowing the real Jesus has huge implications – both for this world and the next.

In the Gospel of Matthew there's a story in which Jesus himself asks whether people have realised who he really is: 'When Jesus came to the region of Caesarea Philippi, he asked his disciples, "Who do people say the Son of Man is?"' (Matthew 16:13).

Firstly, that's a very enigmatic way of talking about yourself, isn't it – Son of Man? The expression comes straight out of a prophecy found in the Old Testament (a prophecy with which his hearers would have been familiar), which spoke of a 'Son of Man' coming with power and glory, beginning a new Kingdom and being someone whom all nations would worship. Jesus is giving them a clue about his significance. His disciples responded, saying, 'Some say John the Baptist; others say Elijah; and still others, Jeremiah or one of the prophets' (Matthew 16:14). In other words, some had confused him with someone else – they had missed who he really was. But then Jesus asks, 'But what about you? Who do you say I am?'

Imagine if Jesus asked that question today – what answers would he get? More to the point, what answer would *you* give?

One answer might be 'baby Jesus' – an infant lying in a manger in a Nativity scene. Perhaps you see him like this – cute but not particularly significant. But is that all that Jesus is?

Or perhaps the answer might be 'good Jesus'. Perhaps you see him as a great moral teacher – like a Ghandi. He certainly did teach some wonderful things. But is that all that Jesus is?

Or the answer might be 'holy Jesus'. Perhaps you see him as a sort of religious guru or prophet – in the same vein as a Confucius or a Mohammed or a Buddha. But is that all that Jesus is?

Or the answer might even be 'legendary Jesus' or 'mythical Jesus'. Perhaps you believe that there might once have been a first-century Jew named Jesus but the whole story about him has been so embellished over the years that it's developed into a myth or legend.

But, the problem with each of these answers is that they simply don't fit the historical record we have about Jesus. Many of the people who were closest to him – who walked with him, talked with him, watched him – knew that he was much more significant than that. In fact, there was little or no confusion in their hearts and minds. It was Peter – speaking for many others – who gave this answer to Jesus' penetrating question: 'You are the Messiah, the Son of the living God' (Matthew 16:16).

The word Peter used means 'anointed one'. In the ancient world, to anoint someone was a way of acknowledging their significance in relation to God. And so Peter was saying loud and clear that this Jesus is a profoundly significant person – that in him we are actually meeting God himself in human form. And so Jesus' response to Peter was:

'Blessed are you, Simon son of Jonah, for this was not revealed to you by flesh and blood, but by my Father in heaven' (Matthew 16:17).

Think about that for a moment. Jesus accepted what Peter had said as true and commended him for it. In other words, Jesus is saying, 'You're right, Peter. I'm more than a quaint first-century Jewish carpenter, I'm more than a religious prophet, I'm more than a moral teacher, I'm more than the basis of a myth or legend – in fact, I *am* the Messiah, the Son of the living God.'

And Jesus also makes it clear that realising his true identity and significance is not something we can do ourselves. Only God can reveal God. Only God can open our eyes and open our hearts to see the real Jesus.

Jesus once said, 'I am the way and the truth and the life. No one comes to the Father except through me' (John 14:6). In doing so, he showed us his significance: that he is the way *to* God, he tells us the truth *about* God and he brings us life *from* God.

Many millions of people over many hundreds of years would want to affirm that the real Jesus is far more than you could imagine. He is not an infant; he is God incarnate. He is not a myth; he is the Master. He is not a legend; he is Lord. Don't confuse him with someone else and, above all, don't miss meeting him.

About twenty-seven years ago I met a young lady at a student conference in Canberra, the capital city of Australia – her name was Belinda. She was gorgeous. I was introduced to her but I felt that she was bit aloof and I mentally dismissed her as I felt she had dismissed me. A year later I found myself at the same conference but this time it was in Melbourne. I met Belinda again and I remembered her as the aloof woman from a year before. But, over the ensuing days, I realised to my horror that I had completely misread her – I had been so wrong that I nearly missed meeting the real Belinda. What I had interpreted as aloofness was, in fact, the exact opposite. I had thought she was one thing but came to realise she was so much more. And I also had no idea of her potential significance to me until, two years later, she became my wife! I am so glad I met the real Belinda.

Today, you are invited to meet the real Jesus – he's more than you can imagine.

Dr Haydn Nelson is married to Belinda and serves as Senior Minister of Riverview Church – a large, contemporary and multi-sited church in Perth, Western Australia (see www.riverviewchurch.com.au). He also holds a PhD in Theology, and has published on the doctrines of Trinity and Providence.

THE GIFT OF CHRISTMAS UNWRAPPED
Ed Olsworth-Peter

Introduction

Nostalgia is in fashion. Whether it's the cosy log fire of the Victorian parlour, the snowy village carol service of the 1950s or simply settling down to watch your favourite Christmas Santa film. We love to splash around in the past, especially at Christmas, when it was *always* snowing so hard everyone could make a 10ft snowman in their front garden! But why? Because it makes us feel safe and it reminds us of a bygone era when life was simple – with the uncomfortable bits conveniently airbrushed out and forgotten. And yet out of such nostalgia and escapism come the traditions we all love and all love to nurture.

The tradition of giving gifts at Christmas is thought to have originated from the account of the Magi bringing gifts to the Christ-child. However, it appears that it was only in medieval times that the practice of giving a gift to your loved ones at Christmas really took off.

I like to find good presents for people, something that will be the talking point for the rest of the obligatory Christmas family get-together. A 'best results' scenario would be something like: 'That was such a good find!' 'Oh, how clever of you to even think of getting that!' 'Now come on … you must have got that on the Internet?' However, I'm always torn between the joy of the gift and the joy of the gift wrap. I like a gift to look good as it sits patiently under the tree waiting for its big reveal, so good in fact that the casual sitting room passer-by just cannot resist seeing who could have possibly gone to so much trouble. Call me vain – but I'm committed to the task.

The tradition of wrapping your gift has an interesting history. Traditionally, brown paper, string and sealing wax were used. Around the turn of the last century coloured tissue paper was also popular. Then, in 1917, gift wrap as we know it was born. Joyce C. Hall – who with his brothers founded Hallmark – owned a stationery shop in Kansas and the story goes that he ran out of brown and tissue paper. In desperation, they put envelope lining paper in the shop (there was a French tradition of lining an otherwise plain envelope with an ornate coloured design). The sheets of paper sold out and people used it to wrap their gifts. Modern gift wrap as we now know it took off and, with modern printing techniques providing seasonal designs, Christmas gift wrap was born.

Christmas unwrapped

There is often a Christmas Day slump around 3 or 4 p.m. Lunch is over, the gifts have been opened and the excitement of the surprise and anticipation is gone. Not so with God's Christmas present. It's a gift that never leaves us feeling flat. The true gift of Christmas is the birth of Jesus, God's own Son born in human form. God gave the gift of Jesus as the first Christmas gift. But how did God gift wrap him? The wrapping he chose tells us a lot about the gift inside.

1. Wrapped in humanity

The Christmas carols we all know so well tell us much about the Christmas story. A common theme in many carols is about God coming to dwell with us, in human form, born of a virgin. This reveals to us the immense love God has for his world and its inhabitants.

Philippians 2:6–7 echoes this:

> *[Jesus] who, being in very nature God, did not consider equality with God something to be used to his own advantage; rather, he made himself nothing by taking the very nature of a servant, being made in human likeness.*

Jesus had a human gift wrap because God wanted to enter fully into our world and into our lives, and you have to be divinely human and earthly present to do that! And a human mother is vital if you are to be actually and bodily born into our world. But also an untouched mother, revealing the divine miraculous nature of his birth and the heavenly location of his home. And so this was no ordinary gift wrap because he was no ordinary baby!

2. Wrapped in poverty

Many carols also talk about Jesus being born in poverty and being born to die. Why?

The Nativity has been described in many different ways over many centuries. Paintings have depicted a clean, organised, bold-coloured world of the stable. But the reality must have been very different. Sleeping in a cave or stable, having travelled for days and with animals moving around you, would look and smell quite different.

Whether Mary and Joseph were poor and how poor they were is open to discussion. But what's clear is that they weren't wealthy and the king of the universe wasn't born into a palace with all the fineries of privilege. 'For you know the grace of our Lord Jesus Christ, that though he was rich, yet for your sake he became poor, so that you through his poverty might become rich' (2 Corinthians 8:9).

The poverty of what Jesus was physically wrapped in is significant. Jesus was wrapped in swaddling bands. Some say swaddling bands were strips of cast-off clothing that the very poor would use to wrap their babies in. Others say they could have been strips of linen taken from material always carried on a long journey in case of a death of one of the party en route, so the body could be wrapped and buried. Similar to the Magi's gift of myrrh, this speaks of the child born to die. The reason for his birth was to save the world from its rebellion and rejection of God. He became poor by taking our sinfulness upon himself, wrapping our sins around him. Not the gift wrap of a king, and yet only the King of kings could allow himself to be wrapped in this way. And yet through his poverty we can become rich because he brings us forgiveness and a new relationship with God.

A final image that sums up the gift wrap of God's Christmas gift is the envelope with a fine French lining. A plain exterior that looks fairly similar to another; the humanity of Christ, all human, but with a dazzling interior of colour and beauty, totally unique and splendid: the divine splendour and radiance, all God.

This is the Christmas celebration! The wonder and glory of God on earth, now gloriously and powerfully resurrected.

Let us be more aware of our humanity as God's creation and more aware of the poverty of our lives without him. This Christmas, unwrap the gift of God again and take a moment to reflect on the wrapping paper of humanity and poverty, receiving this gift in a whole new way. Let us celebrate by receiving Jesus, the earthly gift from heaven, and by wrapping ourselves in Jesus as he wrapped himself in us.

Revd Ed Olsworth-Peter is a creative communicator and is interested in the active relationship between the arts, media and Christian faith. He has worked as a chaplain in two of London's West End theatres and is a council member of the Actors Church Union. He worked for a fresh expression of church in central London exploring journeys of faith through stories of creation and is also a writer and composer. Ed is currently Vicar of two Anglican churches in South East London, one exploring what it means to be an 'Urban Village' and the other developing the use of the creative arts to engage the wider community with its resident creative professionals. For more details, see www.holytrinitycentre.org.uk and www.augustineonetreehill.org.uk. Ed is married to Lisa who is a professional performer and vocal coach in London.

CHRISTMAS EVE
Paul Perkin

Isaiah foretells the good news of the birth of a child, but a birth that was the most costly in history:

> *For to us a child is born, to us a son is given,*
> *and the government will be on his shoulders.*
> *And he will be called Wonderful Counsellor, Mighty God,*
> *Everlasting Father, Prince of Peace.* (Isaiah 9:6)

Think back to 1940: the country is in chaos, the British army is retreating to Dunkirk, invasion is certain and imminent. Supplies are low, food is scarce and morale is rock-bottom. Ammunition stores are empty, there is absolutely no defence against the invader and the country is staring defeat in the face. And at the front door of No. 10 Downing Street a man with rather an odd appearance arrives, demanding an audience with Winston Churchill. 'I must speak to the Prime Minister! I have the answer! The enemy will not conquer – the invasion will be repelled! I've got the secret of victory!' The policeman outside No. 10 has a cynical smirk on his face. What exactly is his hidden weapon? Can he bring America into the war? Has he developed a super-bomb? What exactly is his solution to the national crisis? 'No, no,' replies the man. 'I've got it! The answer is … a baby!'

Well, I don't think he'd have got very far into No. 10, do you? And I wonder what reception Isaiah got to his message in 734 BC – no less a national crisis, as the Assyrian army advanced south, destroying every town and city in Samaria in its path. 'A baby's going to be born! That will be the answer.'

What Isaiah saw, however, is that this baby would be no ordinary child. What Isaiah also faintly saw was that this prediction was looking forward to the birth of not just a special leader, but a unique one in the history of the world. You see, each of the four descriptions of him combine a special but natural human character with an extraordinary, in fact supernatural, quality. What we have then are four human characters, people with special – but at the end of the day natural – roles:

- the counsellor (the wise person)
- the powerful person of influence
- the father
- and the person with nobility and status, the prince.

Used rightly, these characteristics hold a family, a community or even a nation, together. And we all need people who make wise judgements, who know how to exercise power for the good of all, who can model the basic family structure that holds society together, people of reputation who use their status responsibly. And Isaiah saw them all rolled into one person.

But there's more. Isaiah put an adjective in front of each character that lifts them out of the purely human into the divine:

- Not just a counsellor, but a miracle-working one!
- Not just a potentate, but a divine one!
- Not just a father, but an everlasting one!
- Not just a prince, but one who can bring world peace!

Jesus is all of these. He fed a multitude, and he can meet our needs. He drove out evil, and he can purify our hearts. He healed the sick and he can touch our bodies. He raised the dead, and he can take us through death into life beyond. Jesus is the wonderful, the wonder-working Counsellor.

He's the divine Power. Human power corrupts, and absolute power tends to corrupt absolutely but there is one who defies that tendency, the one who is divine power – he will never abuse his power over us. We are safe in his hands. Jesus is the divine Power.

He's the everlasting Father. Because we think of Jesus as the Son of God, and therefore in a sense our brother, we forget that he also models the compassion and strength of fatherhood. No one has ever been a 100 per cent faithful, ever-loving, always consistent, always there kind of father. But if we have become one of God's family, the Bible says he will never leave us or forsake us; 'Jesus Christ is the same yesterday and today and for ever' (Hebrews 13:8). So don't dwell too long on the baby in the manger. Jesus is the everlasting Father.

And he's the peace-making Prince. There are a few princes in our royal family and they do lots of very good work. They oil the wheels of international relations, of world trade and of political negotiation. But they can't bring world peace. It's asking too much. But the whole government is on Jesus' shoulders: he's the Prime Minister, the Chancellor of the Exchequer, the Home Secretary, the Foreign Secretary and the whole cabinet rolled into one – and he's the key to world peace. Jesus is the Prince of Peace.

Perhaps you think he's not making a very good job of it! He's had 2,000 years in government, but the world doesn't seem to be much better governed or more peaceful as a result. There is still war and enmity, especially in the part of the world where he was born!' Nevertheless:

One day he will bring peace. One day in the future he will create universal peace – the issue is one of timing. One day he will rule the universe visibly. The following chapters in Isaiah are all about that: 'for the earth will be filled with the knowledge of the LORD as the waters cover the sea' (Isaiah 11:9).

One day he did bring peace. One day in the past he made the most important peace that we need – peace with God. Imagine as he grew up to become a carpenter, what he took on his shoulder: timber from the timber yard to his carpenter's shop. And thirty years after his birth, he took on his shoulder the two beams of a cross, and was crucified on it. The Good News day of his birth at Christmas looked forward to the Good News day when he took our sin and separation from God. That's why we call it Good Friday. When he carried our sins to the cross, he took the government of the world on his shoulders. So we celebrate his birth by remembering his death.

And one day he does bring peace. Any day in the present, he makes peace starting with each of us individually – if we will allow him. He re-unites us with God when we welcome him into our lives, and that's the start of reconciled human relations on earth. The fact that the world is in many places still at war is simply a sign that they haven't submitted to the Prince of Peace.

Revd Paul Perkin is married to Christine, the father of three children in their twenties, and guardian of a Yamaha sports bike. Previously a physicist and teacher, since ordination in the Church of England he has served in a dockyard parish, and then at Holy Trinity Brompton, where he was also chaplain of the Brompton Hospital. Together with Christine, Paul led a church plant at St Mark's Battersea Rise, and sent plants to regenerate other churches in Balham and in Battersea. They are leaders in the New Wine network, and authors of *Parenting Teenagers* (Kingsway, 2007).

PEACE *(SHALOM)* ON EARTH: THE MESSAGE OF THE SEASON!

Susan Perlman

Peace. Everybody is for it. Nobody is against it. As we enter this season of celebrating the One who is the *Sar Shalom* (Prince of Peace), it begs the question, 'What is that very elusive quality we call peace?' It means different things to different people.

Peace is what those who follow Eastern religions say comes only through the obliteration of the individual personality, becoming a part of the universe with no awareness of self. But what they really mean is serenity.

Peace is what the elderly couple want when the teenager next door is practising on his drums. They really want quiet.

Peace is what the shopkeeper wants when he's worried about paying his bills. He really means that he'd like his store to be busy and bustling with customers over the Christmas holiday. Peace to him means prosperity.

The patient waiting anxiously in the doctor's office to be told the results of a battery of lab tests wants peace. She really means good health.

When we don't have what we think we should have, we say we need peace! So 'peace' is often defined as the condition of life that *should* be. But who has the right to determine what should or shouldn't be? If all of us could get the kind of peace we wanted, it would be an imposed peace. It would be peace at the expense of someone else's dream of what peace should be. Peace cannot be determined by our own biased viewpoints or selfish needs. Nor can our standard for peace be set by the norms of our turbulent society. So where can we look, if not to ourselves or society? How do we set up criteria for defining 'peace'?

Dictionary definitions centre around two major themes. One deals with the cessation of hostilities, the other focuses on a freedom from inner turmoil, better known as peace of mind. The word, as commonly used in English, comes from the Latin *pax*. *Pax* to the Romans meant a cessation of hostilities between the conqueror and the vanquished. This peace was always temporary because it depended on who was in the position of strength. However, the ancient Hebrew concept of peace, rooted in the word *shalom*, meant wholeness, completeness, soundness, health, safety and prosperity – carrying with it the implication of permanence.

The criteria for *shalom* – true peace – rests with God and the first example of peace in the Bible is the condition that existed in the beginning in Eden. The Genesis account of creation demonstrates peace. Adam and Eve were at peace with God and all he created. Their needs were supplied. They did not suffer hunger, disease or pain of any kind. Beauty surrounded them so that they could experience and enjoy it. They weren't lonely, for they had each other and, more importantly, they had an intimate relationship with their Creator. If any people ever experienced peace, it was Adam and Eve. The condition of peace existed in the garden only as long as they were obedient to God's will. Unfortunately, they disobeyed and the *shalom* of God was lost for them. But if, through Adam and Eve, we see that peace was lost through disobedience, in Abraham we see the opposite:

> Then God said, 'Take your son, your only son, whom you love – Isaac – and go to the region of Moriah. Sacrifice him there as a burnt offering on a mountain that I will show you.' Early the next morning Abraham got up and loaded his donkey. He took with him two of his servants and his son Isaac. When he had cut enough wood for the burnt offering, he set out for the place God had told him about. (Genesis 22:2–3)

It seems beyond the comprehension of most people to follow such instructions, let alone to do so without anger, anxiety or despair. But Abraham obeyed God. He recognised that God had the right to require Isaac's life if he so chose. This trust and reliance in the One who created him made it possible for Abraham to have peace of mind, even when all his natural senses must have told him otherwise.

Peace, lasting peace, transcends the situations and flaws of our own personal lives because it doesn't come from us. We spend countless millions of pounds and an endless amount of effort to negotiate between people and nations today. We act as though peace could be achieved through social or political solutions. Yet our world is a hotbed of warring. Even Jerusalem (the name means City of Peace) is a place where acts of terrorism abound.

So should we just pack it in? Absolutely not. The peace that we long for is not based on political compromises or even humanitarian efforts, no matter how noble they might be; real peace is based on righteousness and truth. The only real peace, the only real *shalom* that is permanent, comes from God.

The Jewish sages teach that when the Messiah comes, there will be peace in the world. They taught that the Messiah is God's solution for peace. The phrase 'when the Messiah comes' is synonymous with 'when peace comes'. The long-held hope for peace would be fulfilled in a person. God promises all the qualities of *shalom* – wholeness, completeness, soundness, health, safety – to those who will look to him. And that is why peace on earth *can* be a reality in your heart this season. Two thousand years ago, a Jewish carpenter we know as Jesus claimed to be that Messiah. He claimed to be the bearer of peace. The peace that Jesus offers us is a peace not based on outward circumstances but on the reality of a restored relationship with the God of Israel. God himself became one of us because he chose to demonstrate his love as the way of peace.

We say we need peace, but are we willing to accept the One who paid the price for us? This Christmas embrace Jesus as your Prince of Peace.

Susan Perlman is the Associate Executive Director of Jews for Jesus and oversees the organisation's communications department (see www.jewsforjesus.org). An accomplished writer and speaker, she came to faith in Jesus through an encounter with Christian rock musician, Larry Norman. Susan is from Brooklyn, New York and was raised in the Orthodox Jewish tradition. Susan was an advertising copywriter and social activist, before moving to San Francisco to become one of Jews for Jesus' founders. She is a contributor to ISSUES, an evangelistic journal for Jewish seekers, and serves on key boards concerned with missions and theological education.

CAN YOU FIND GOD?
John Peters

Can you find God? Or is he lost like the soap, misplaced like the car keys, concealing himself like a giggling child in a cosmic game of hide-and-seek? Is God far too distant to get personally involved? Or is he so personally involved that any fool can find him, provided they are willing to look within? Is he as instantly available as a cappuccino on a city street or do you have to strive for ever to attain him?

Is he merely a myth, the mother of all tooth fairies, whom we've largely grown out of? Is he anything more than an echo from the voice of the world in her youth? Is he an exercise in wish fulfilment for those in need of an emotional crutch – to get them through the struggles of this life?

Can you find God? Can you find him when you're at the office, can you find him when you're on the tube, when you're out buying gloves, when you're home making love?

Can you find God? When there are storms and droughts and floods? When innocent children are murdered, when there are terrorist attacks and wars?

Some may ask, 'How can you *not* find God?' in the apparent evidence of design and order in the universe. I went to the Houston Space Center and the man who showed us around had worked during his career with the astronauts who went on all the major space missions. I asked him what they believed about God. He said that all the astronauts he knew were believers because of the evidence of intelligent design. For them, this evidence included facts such as, if the sun was just a little nearer to the earth we would fry and that if it was just a little further away we would freeze.

Can you find God? When you feel the power of the waves, see heart-stopping vistas of natural beauty or hear from those who have had astonishing experiences on the shadowy border between life and death? Can we find God in the universal human drive to invest life with meaning and purpose, to adhere to some kind of moral order or even in the very need to ask these kinds of questions at all? Questions that disturb neither elephants nor ants? *We* are the asking animal, being possessed of a questioning, curious spirit that disturbs us within, pushing us to search for answers. Why is that?

If there is a God, would you want to find him? Are you bothered? Life is so busy. Perhaps you don't think he's put in much of an appearance so far. Maybe you feel he's underperformed. Maybe you aren't sure you want him to find you – or perhaps you aren't convinced he'd be interested in finding you.

Can you find God? All the great thinkers have wrestled with this question: Confucius, Mohammed, Buddha and Ghandi. Surely, it's a question everyone asks at some stage.

This is the Christmas question, of course – possibly more critical than whether or not you'll get a turkey leg, the latest PlayStation, that darling pair of shoes or a new iPhone.

What if God was one of us? Collapsing himself somehow into a cradle, like a skyscraper fitting itself into a matchbox? Making himself ridiculously vulnerable to us in the blood and sweat of the birth process? In the filth of a stable? In a carpenter's shop? In a succession of peasant villages, under a Roman sky, in one of the most controversial countries on earth?

What if the question, 'Can you find God?' has already been answered some 2,000 years ago? Has anyone else lived a life like Jesus of Nazareth, taught as he taught, performed the extraordinary acts he's said to have done? What if he really made God discoverable, revealed him in the disposable clothing of flesh and blood? What if he came as a baby to attract us and not as a galactic superpower to impress or overwhelm us because that's the kind of God he is – a kind God?

What if he lived with the knowledge that a day would come when he would have to walk right into the eye of the storm, allowing himself to be stretched out on an agony of unforgiving wood? What if he chose to enter into our death not because he was a fool, a martyr or a hero but because by doing so he knew he could draw the sting of death itself? What if death could not hold him and he was raised from the dead? Does this not mean that he is the possessor of all the answers, the Lord of life, making other theories about him (good man, wise man, teacher man, thief) way too small?

What if this is the most important thing the world has ever heard? That I will ever hear in my life? More important than news from the financial markets or news from the person I love?

Revd John Peters is Rector of St Mary's, Bryanston Square, a church in central London with an average age of 26 (see www.stmaryslondon.com). After graduating in Law and then studying Theology at Wycliffe College, Oxford, John and his wife Jenny started St Mary's as a new church congregation in 2000. Since then, they have planted six churches here and overseas. John and Jenny have three children.

THE BEST CHRISTMAS PRESENT EVER
David C.L. Prior

I have discovered a lot of interesting – and many more useless – facts about the Christmas story. One of the discussions I heard was an interview with the Archbishop of Canterbury on BBC Radio 5. He was asked whether the story of the three wise men is true. He answered that the story is essentially accurate, as he believes it, but that all sorts of legends have grown up around it. One is that there were *three* wise men, because in the text of Matthew's Gospel it never says that; it simply says there were three gifts presented to the baby when the kings – the wise men, or literally the Magi, magicians or astrologers – arrived in Bethlehem.

These men were wealthy people who travelled a long distance to find a baby whose birth had been heralded for them by a special star. They took a lot of time, faced a lot of dangers on the way, had to negotiate the particularly cruel viciousness of Herod in Jerusalem, and they came to search for this baby because, they said, 'We want to worship him.' At the end of that particular story we read that 'they bowed down and worshipped [Jesus]' (Matthew 2:11). Then they offered him gifts of gold, frankincense and myrrh.

There have been many conclusions drawn from that narrative. There is something about the three wise men that grabs our attention. When they arrived in Jerusalem, their question was, 'Where is he?' I think that is very often where we arrive on Christmas Eve, wanting to find Jesus and asking not just one, but many questions. But what is it that the wise men registered when they arrived at the stable in Bethlehem and saw the child with his mother? What led them to worship him? Why had they chosen and why did they offer these particular gifts? I think the best way to understand this is in the carol 'We Three Kings of Orient Are'. Written by John Hopkins in 1857, it was intended for a Christmas pageant. As a theologian and a professor in a seminary, he dwells on the visitation of the three Magi and he puts words on the lips of each king.

> *Born a King on Bethlehem's plain,*
> *Gold I bring to crown him again,*
> *King for ever, ceasing never,*
> *Over us all to reign.*

This one of the Magi saw in the baby a king, not just another king and not a king like King Herod, but the King who was to reign over all of us … and so the gift he brought was gold, symbolising royalty.

When we think of the gold presented to Jesus, there is in that gift a mirror into our own lives – are we ready to worship our king, the King of kings and Lord of lords? And will we allow that king to work on us? To him we are like gold. He loves us so much, so intensely, so profoundly and so internally that he never lets us go and never gives up on us. And we are to him 'rebellious gold', because we don't really like him to take too much interest in us. Will we crown Jesus king of our lives and let the king deal with the 'rebellious gold' that remains within each of us? That's what th first gift says to me.

The second one, in the words of John Hopkins, goes like this:

> *Frankincense to offer have I;*
> *Incense owns a Deity nigh;*
> *Prayer and praising, voices raising,*
> *Worshipping God on high.*

In other words, as that king prostrated himself before the baby, he saw not just an earthly king, but God in the flesh. God with us – Emmanuel. That led him to offer frankincense, as fuel for prayer and praise. The Christmas story is full of praise: the praise of the angels; the shepherds praising God; Mary praising God. And to worship Jesus is to be released into praise that is totally non-self-centred. It is where we are turned away from ourselves and into the supreme activity for which we have been created – to praise Almighty God. The story of the three wise men is precisely one of God coming among us, being one with us, taking our human nature in all its vulnerability and saying, 'I love you enough to come alongside you and invite your worship, so that I can release you into praise.'

The third gift was myrrh. Myrrh occurs on two other occasions in the Gospels and both have to do with the death of Jesus. When he was hanging on the cross, the soldiers offered him a cup of sour wine mixed with myrrh, because myrrh was a drug that would have reduced the pain. Jesus refused it. The other occasion is when Joseph of Arimathea and Nicodemus take the body of Jesus down from the cross for burial. They covered the body in spices and the one that is mentioned particularly is myrrh. I believe those realities led John Hopkins to write this:

> Myrrh is mine; its bitter perfume
> Breathes a life of gathering gloom;
> Sorrowing, sighing, bleeding, dying,
> Sealed in the stone cold tomb.

The gift of myrrh, turned around to be a mirror into our lives, is asking us to take sin seriously. God took it so seriously that he sent his Son to die for us. The myrrh should remind us that, 'the wages of sin is death, but the gift of God is eternal life in Christ Jesus our Lord' (Romans 6:23). So, this particular gift opens up the way to eternal life.

These are some of the realities the three wise men open up for us. He is King and the man offered him gold. Will we crown him King of our lives and let him deal with the 'rebellious gold' within us?

The second wise man offered frankincense to show he saw in the baby God Almighty in the flesh and it released him into worship and praise. Are we ready for that at the start of this Christmas?

And the third wise man offered myrrh because he saw through the birth and through the life to the death on a hill, on a cross surrounded by two others; and in his death Jesus has brought us life.

Thank you, God, for giving us Jesus. He's the best possible gift.

Revd David Prior and his wife Rosemary live a double life – six months looking after a church in Florida, six months at home in West Sussex, England. Over the last forty-five years they have been involved with churches in Surrey, Cape Town, Oxford, London and Washington DC. For five years (1995–2000) David concentrated on ministry in the workplace in London, both in the West End and the City. He is the author of *Joel, Micah, Habakkuk* and *1 Corinthians*, both in The Bible Speaks Today series. They have four children and seven grandchildren.

FESTIVE RUBBISH
Mark Ritchie

Are you feeling Christmassy yet? Kids can often get us into the Christmas mood. I heard Naomi (13 years old) give some good advice about asking for a gift. She said, 'If you want a kitten, start off by asking for a horse.' Mind you, my favourite piece of kids' advice is from Laura who said, 'When your mum is mad at your dad, don't let her brush your hair.'

As I was growing up, Christmas mornings were all very similar: everyone had their different jobs to do. The children's job was to rip open every present as quickly as possible. My mum's job was to try and remember who had given us what. My dad's job was to wander around the room in his pyjamas carrying a big bin bag and collecting all the wrapping paper. One year, my younger sister got a doll; I distinctly remember it smelling of strawberries! Around 11 a.m. my grandparents arrived and, as always, we had to show off our favourite presents. So us boys gathered our things and my sister went to find her new doll to be displayed and sniffed, but it was nowhere to be found! After a thorough interrogation my parents *finally* believed that I had not touched the doll. You have no idea how much happiness it brought me when my dad eventually found the doll in the bin bag out the back with the rubbish. My dad had thrown the gift out with the wrapping!

There is a lot of wrapping around Christmas and sometimes it's difficult to know what to throw away and what to keep. It's really easy for our attention to be grabbed by all the glittery, shiny packaging of Christmas so that we miss the true gift, the thing it's really all about.

When my son Jordan was 5 years old we bought him some goalposts for Christmas. As a lazy dad the extent of my effort would have been to wrap them up in Christmas paper, but my wife had other ideas. So there I was on a rainy Christmas Eve in the back garden putting up goalposts. Entering into the spirit of things and wanting to make it special, my finishing touch was to put the football right in front of the goal. I could just see my little son running downstairs and out into the garden where his first act on Christmas Day would be to score a goal.

In the morning he rushed downstairs as planned and saw the living room full of presents. I was so excited to tell him that it got even better! I took him into the back garden, where everything was set ready for him to kick the ball straight into the net. I will never forget his reaction as he pointed at the goal and said, 'I did not want that!'

You might be laughing at his reaction, but we all know what it's like to get unwanted gifts. If you've ever received a soap-on-a-rope you know what I'm talking about. You probably even have a special face for receiving unwanted gifts – the smile that almost ends up as a grimace as you attempt to conceal your despair!

I find it fascinating that Christmas has become linked to unwanted gifts. The Bible says that God gave Jesus as a gift and the people of the time did not want the present. It says in John 3:16, 'For God so loved the world that he gave his one and only Son …' When we read the Bible we see that the people of that time were looking for a Messiah, a revolutionary who would overthrow the government and become their new leader. They did not want this Jesus who came and loved the outcasts, healed the sick and spoke of loving your enemies. In fact, they pinned him to a cross, an act which shouted, 'We did not want that!'

Even today we look around us and see financial challenges, family breakdowns and the stresses of life and we question the gift that God has given us. We wonder what relevance a little baby in a manger has to our lives today. By taking a closer look at the gift of Jesus we can realise that what God has given us is a bridge. God sent Jesus as a bridge between us and him. The Bible says that things have come between us and God. Sin is like a chasm and there is nothing we can do to get over that. Yet God has made a way by sending his Son to die on the cross so that we can be connected to him.

I always think of the scene at the end of *I'm a Celebrity, Get Me Out Of Here*. You know, the bit at the end where the B-list celeb has finished their stint in the jungle and is allowed to cross the bridge, usually amid fireworks, into the open arms of their loved ones. Jesus is the bridge that we cross into the arms of our loving heavenly Father. God is looking for you. He wants to embrace you. The true gift of Christmas is God sending his Son so that we could connect with him. The whole of John 3:16 says this: 'For God so loved the world that he gave his one and only Son, that whoever believes in him shall not perish but have eternal life.'

Don't make the mistake my dad made with the strawberry doll! Don't throw away the true gift of Christmas with the wrapping.

Mark Ritchie is a creative communicator of the gospel, who has travelled extensively through the UK and overseas. He combines humorous storytelling with a passion that has impacted tens of thousands in a transforming way. For more information on 73rd Trust, the ministry base for Mark Ritchie, visit www.73rdtrust.com.

YOU CAN'T ALWAYS GET WHAT YOU WANT; BUT YOU GET WHAT YOU NEED

Chris Russell

I know it's the season of peace and goodwill and all that, and I don't want to be the bringer of bad news, but … you don't need *any* of the things you will get for Christmas. Neither will you give anything that is needed. Not really needed. If we just skipped the present-exchanging of Christmas would we truly be any poorer for it? Our lives are so full already. So full, but so unfulfilled.

In such full lives it can seem as if God doesn't particularly add a different dynamic. We are surrounded by a story that has become very familiar – from wearing tea towels and dressing gowns as the shepherds, through to having the songs as a soundtrack playing in the background as we queue to buy presents. Yes, somewhere in our minds is the connection that we give gifts to each other because at Christmas we celebrate God giving us the gift of Jesus – but if he is just like these other gifts, it isn't going to make a real difference, is it?

And because we don't need anything we get at Christmas, we may assume there is nothing here we really, truly need – it's simply a story that we like. And so to those of us whose hands and cupboards are so full already the urgency of the gift of Christmas can seem like another of those things we know might just make life 'nicer'.

But what if this all-too-familiar narrative, instead of providing the white noise for the activities of acquiring more stuff we don't need, actually addresses us with the greatest truth, showing us most starkly and decisively what it is that we *do* need. And showing it to us by giving it to us.

Christmas addresses what we need – not by offering us an idea of what could be, what might be possible, what could be a new outlook or a new option. Christmas doesn't create in us a new understanding of what we need, and leave us to struggle and search to have that need met. No, it's a place where the deepest and profoundest needs of every human are revealed – and met.

We all have the bits of the Christmas story we like the most, the lines of the carols that move our hearts, the themes that resonate with us. But as rich as this story is in these connections, if we just look at these bits we miss out. Because they are all pointing to a baby. A screaming, sleeping, vulnerable, needy, new-born child.

What if this one, freshly born human being teaches us what we need. What if this gift *is* what we need. All of us. Whether we like it or not. A gift that changes everything. That creates the alternative. That doesn't just open up the potential of something new, but actualises that new thing. There is too much to say about this – it is a bit like holding a cup under the Niagara Falls and trying to capture what is going on. So one sentence will do – words spoken by the angels to the shepherds:

> *Do not be afraid. I bring you good news that will cause great joy for all the people. Today in the town of David a Saviour has been born to you; he is the Messiah, the Lord.* (Luke 2:10–11)

We know fear is rampant around us and in us. We know that having more things we don't need doesn't reduce our fear – in fact it increases. What is it that we are most afraid of? Which of us is fearful for those we love? Whose fears for their children keep them awake late and stir them early from sleep? Who is fearful about health? Who is fearful of the future and the unknown? Who fears work – is it that your job is not secure, is it that it is not fulfilling and you fear life slipping through your hands? What about money and security? Whose daily fears are over relationships and love? Is it that the relationship you most desire might never be, or is it that a relationship you are in is everything you didn't want it to be? Who looks ahead and sees the fear of death?

Tom Wright observes that the most regularly given command by God in Scripture is, 'Do not fear, do not be afraid …' How wonderful! What great news. The only drawback being that we haven't got a clue how to obey it.

To my shame I think that sometimes I have given the impression that we needn't fear because bad things don't happen. That God will keep us from the things that we fear. That they won't come to pass. But that's not true. No, these words aren't spoken to us because fear isn't to be feared. Quite simply, we need not fear because we are not alone. Whatever we face, whatever comes to pass, we are not left solitary. Our greatest fear is that we are alone. That there is no one really with us, for us, by our side.

'Does anyone understand what I am going through? Is anyone in this with me?' Christmas says a gentle and irrepressible, 'yes'. Jesus is.

This is what we really need to know – that we never face the hardest things in life alone. God is present to his world. God comes to us. At huge personal cost and risk, with the most profound consequences to himself. But God comes to this earth, to this people, and he comes as one who is with us and for us. And when God comes to us, he comes not to be convinced about us, not to check our behaviour and weigh up his decision, not to gather evidence against us to put before a jury who might condemn us. He comes with his mind made up. With the verdict clear and certain. He comes as Saviour.

This is what we need. We can't save ourselves. And he comes to the earth as Saviour. Not just to some people, but everyone. To you in the situation of your life, as you are now, not as you would be, but as you are now – to you he comes as Saviour.

But here is news that is addressed to every single person. This is a direct message. The angel of the Lord points directly to you and to me, individually, yet he addresses us together. He does this for each of us. And this news ties us together as brothers and sisters who share a wonderful gift from their Father. No one is first, no one is last, no one gets preference, no one is missed out, not a single one is neglected. This gift is given to each and every one. Here – direct from his hands – hands so tiny on his birth night, yet hands that will one day be split in two by nails – here we get what we desperately need. Take it, won't you?

Revd Chris Russell is proud to call Reading his home; he lives there with his wife Belinda and three daughters. He is vicar of St Laurence, a church in the centre of the town which lives and breathes to see young people come to faith and live the faith. He is increasingly convinced and passionate that the local church is God's primary instrument in personal and public transformation. His first book, *Ten Letters: to be Opened in the Event of My Death*, was published this year.

THE FOUR Cs OF CHRISTMAS
Mark Russell

There was a little boy in Dublin, who was very impatient to have a new bike for Christmas. 'Mum … you know how Christmas is Jesus' birthday? I think Jesus would want me to be happy on his birthday, and so I should have a new bike.' His mother was a good Christian woman and she replied, 'I think Jesus would be really upset you are using his birthday to get a new bike. No, you are not getting one!'

The following morning when she came down to breakfast, she looked over and saw the little Nativity set. But it didn't look right, something was missing! She looked more closely. On the spot where Mary should have been was a little piece of paper. She opened it and there in her son's distinctive handwriting were the words, 'Dear Jesus, if you wanna see your mum again, make sure I get my bike on Christmas Day!'

We may laugh, but for many it sums up the meaning of Christmas. Expensive gifts, big bills, lots of food, too much drink.

In the seven days running up to Christmas, Asda estimates it will have sold 750,000 tonnes of Christmas pudding: that is the weight of 1,876 jumbo jets. Marks & Spencer estimates that it will sell more than 500 tonnes of sprouts over the Christmas period: that is as heavy as 125 double-decker buses. And if all the Christmas crackers sold by Tesco in a year were laid end to end, they would stretch for 3,082 miles – the length of the entire UK coastline.

Over Christmas the UK population will consume almost 5.5 million jars of mincemeat, 12 million jars of pickles and 6.5 million jars of cranberry sauce all packaged in glass, but only a small percentage of that glass will get recycled. And if all these glass jars *were* recycled, it would save enough energy to boil water for 60 million cups of tea.

Royal Mail delivers around 550 million cards and packets during the pre-Christmas period. It is estimated that up to 1 billion Christmas cards (17 for every man, woman and child) could end up afterwards in bins across the UK. If all these cards were laid end to end they would span from London to Sydney and back more than five times!

Over 6 million Christmas trees were bought in the UK, and most of them were thrown away afterwards, creating over 9,000 tonnes of additional rubbish, almost five times the weight of the London Eye. It is estimated that over Christmas as much as 83 square kilometres of wrapping paper will end up in Greater London rubbish bins, enough to cover Hyde Park 33 times!

Is this Christmas? For many people, Christmas is a stressful time. Is this what Christmas is all about? This is Jesus' birthday, and for many people Jesus will not even get an invitation to his own party. Jesus is being airbrushed out of Christmas. Over half of my Christmas cards said 'Seasons Greetings', 'Happy Holiday' or 'Cool Yule'. Let's not have a happy Xmas either, let's have a wonderful happy CHRISTmas.

Christmas begins with a C. Let me give you four Cs to sum up this awesome story:

Cradle

God sent his only Son into this world 2,000 years ago. He was not born in luxury or splendour; he was born in a stable and laid in a manger. God himself took part in the mystery of human birth. Yet I think we have sanitised Christmas. Can you imagine giving birth in those conditions, not an epidural in sight! Cold air, damp straw, animal poo everywhere. We make the manger scene all cute and lovely … We are all familiar with the cute Christmas Nativity scene, but Jesus didn't stay in a manger.

Cross

He grew up, he went about the country, he did good, he healed the sick, he raised the dead, he gave sight to the blind and he fed the hungry. He said radical and awesome things that millions of people today still live their lives by. Jesus never owned an office, never wrote a book, never got a university degree, never owned a house; in fact, he never travelled more than 200 miles from the place of his birth. He did none of the things we associate with power and importance. And when he was in his early thirties, he died on a cross, his death paying the price of our sin, our wrongs.

But he rose again from the dead. The grave is empty, Jesus is alive.

Crown

He is the King of kings, the Lord of lords, the Prince of Peace. He is the God who didn't just stay in heaven and tell us he loved us through a loudhailer. He was born into this world, he walked this earth, because he loved each of us. Even if it was just for you, he would still have come to the earth. What a thought! That is how awesome God thinks you are, how special you are to him. He loves you more than words can say.

This Christmas, God offers you a present. God offers each of us a present. Not a present you will lose interest in by tomorrow. He offers us Jesus. He offers us that peace that this world cannot offer. He offers us the unconditional love of the God who made us. He offers us a relationship, he offers us the knowledge that the God of heaven is just a prayer away to help us and sustain us, he offers us the surety that we will go to heaven. Quite simply ... he offers us life. This leads me to the last C.

Choice

This Christmas, I challenge you. Don't just let the story of Christmas be a cute little story. Allow the wonder, the joy, the mystery of Christmas to enter your life and change you. Christmas is about Christ – his cradle, his cross, his crown and our choice.

Canon Mark Russell is the Chief Executive of Church Army, a movement of over 300 evangelists who work across the UK and Ireland (see www.churcharmy.org.uk). He has led missions across the world and is a regular contributor to the media. In his spare time he loves travelling, skiing and the gym.

STAND UP TO RECEIVE THE GIFT OF CHRISTMAS

Tim Saiet

For some, the struggles and issues of life, controlled and buried in their hearts throughout the year, surface as Christmas approaches and Christmas is about survival. But however you see Christmas, something hugely significant happened in Bethlehem about two thousand years ago. Because of the birth of Jesus, God has something significant for us as we journey together.

In Proverbs, we read:

> *Trust in the LORD with all your heart and lean not on your own understanding; in all your ways submit to him, and he will make your paths straight.* (Proverbs 3:5–6)

Trusting in the Lord with all your heart is easily said but hard to do, because our ability to trust is shaped by our experience. But God asks us to lay down our experience and trust him in a way we might never have done before. In these words we can see that when we trust the Lord with *all* of our hearts we are not to lean on our own education, upbringing, knowledge, experience, teaching, ability, courage, strength, persistence, accomplishments or power. Then anything is possible – God can shape our future in a way we might never have imagined. He is *that* powerful and full of love. And this is the God we trust.

In the New Testament we see a man who was an invalid for thirty-eight years (John 5:1–9). He was disabled and in those days you needed friends and family to carry you around if you could not use crutches. Life was hard and the likelihood of this man being healed was slim because of his circumstances. But Jesus is a changer of circumstances. That's how he works. Jesus broke into this man's circumstances and healed him. He met that man there and then and he meets us here and now, where we are, in our own circumstances … Jesus knows our needs before we pray.

Crackers are a Christmas favourite in the UK. They were first made in 1850 by a London sweet-maker called Tom Smith. One night, sitting in front of his crackling log fire, watching the sparks, he thought what fun it would be if his sweets and toys could be opened with a crack when their wrappers were pulled in half. Today's Christmas cracker evolved from this and has three things: a hat, a joke or message and a present.

The hat

This is not just a hat but is actually a crown, the crown of a king. On Christmas Day we celebrate the birth of Jesus born as a king. God came down from heaven and became like man, born a baby, yet those around him knew that he was to be worshipped. For Jesus to make any difference in our lives and for us to have a relationship with him we have to acknowledge that he is the Son of God, that he is a king. He came to rescue us from ourselves. We are incapable of rescuing ourselves so we need a Saviour: a Saviour who knows the troubles of our hearts, a Saviour who knows our pain and who wants to restore us to a relationship with his Father in heaven. So we wear this hat on Christmas Day to remember that a king was born, a Saviour who would die so that humanity could be restored to a loving relationship with its Creator, God himself.

To have this relationship with God we need to keep Proverbs 3:5–6 in mind and remember that he is a God who can do anything he likes in all creation. If we trust him then anything is possible. He knows how to protect us, he knows our needs, he knows our desires and dreams, he knows our brokenness. Jesus experienced brokenness when he was alone on the cross and can identify with our pain, our rejection. The Bible tells us he became a man to experience everything that we experience, so Jesus understands our situation. Jesus wants to keep us safe under his protection and to be our guide, now at Christmas time and beyond, but we need to make a choice. We need to relinquish the desire to control our lives. It won't be easy but, if we dare, we will flourish and step into our full potential.

The message

Cracker jokes can be really corny and fun to read at the table at Christmas, but the real message of Christmas is not a joke, it is one of life-changing, mind-blowing hope. The message of Christmas is the truth that God's Son Jesus came down to earth, and was born as a baby, that we all might know God in a personal and intimate way. That Jesus is the way to a life of fullness and satisfaction. Jesus offers the truth and Jesus shows the way to this new life.

When we accept Jesus, he will restore us to who we really are: human beings whose lives are meant to be lived in a relationship with their Creator. Jesus does the work in us. His message is that God loves us and wants to have a relationship with us. Love is the message of Christmas. Jesus is the messenger.

The gift

We love getting gifts at Christmas. We don't have to earn a gift – it is a way of being blessed by others. But what if someone wanted to give you a gift and to make it the most important gift in your whole life? To make it the most significant and life-changing gift? What if that person had to die to give it to you? Would you be grateful?

Jesus offers us the gift of a new life on earth and also the gift of eternal life. Life as we know it is not the end. Some of us do not want to take the gifts Jesus offers because we fear the unknown. Others fear receiving gifts because those they have received before have come with conditions. Others fear they won't be able to live up to what Jesus asks of them. We may be lame and crippled by the hurts, habits, hang-ups and wounds of the past, or by unbelief, believing in Jesus but following him from a distance, reading the Scriptures but not really believing them fully, not engaging with them in our hearts, not knowing in our hearts that God loves us more than anything else on earth.

Many of us have been hurt and scarred and want to stand up to meet with Jesus, like the man at the pool, but we feel unable to. So we stay seated, as if crippled because of the trial and hurts of life. We end up living defeated lives, fearing success and change. Can we really afford not to stand and respond to Jesus when he asks us, 'Do you want to get well?' 'Do you want to be whole?' Jesus is saying it to us today. He speaks to us as he speaks to that man at the pool: 'Do you want to get well?'

The gift of Christmas is Jesus. Why don't we turn to Jesus, like the man at the pool, and ask him to help us with whatever we need today. Let's not stay seated, let's stand up and receive whatever gifts and blessings Jesus wants to give us today.

Revd Tim Saiet is a creative communicator who combines the powerful message of Jesus with illustrative illusions and creative visual effects. He is married to Charlotte and lives in Harrow, London. Tim is a former Royal Marine Commando and has spent time coaching all types of skiing and outdoor winter pursuits. He has worked in the Arctic Circle and has taught in many ski schools around the world. He has also worked as a life coach and has equipped and trained many different people in the church, and in the corporate market, in how to apply the truths and message of the Christian faith into their lives. Tim has previously spent three years as a church leader in London and has spoken throughout the UK and abroad about the love of God and the mind-blowing transformation that is offered by a relationship with Jesus. For further details, see www.philotrust.com.

THE TRUE CHRISTMAS STORY
David Shearman

How do we think about the coming of Jesus into our world? Whatever our view of the Christmas story, the Bible is incredibly clear that if you understand it, it's not just a story to tell, it's something that requires action.

What did the people who were there think about it? In Nazareth, when Mary started to show a bump, some people said she was having an illegitimate child – and Jesus was spoken of as an illegitimate child in adulthood. Others, particularly Herod and later the Pharisees, saw Jesus as a threat. Most of those who thought about it at all – and the majority didn't think about it at all – didn't understand or know what was going on. They saw the birth of this humble child as just another baby born into a poor home.

What about us? What do we think? Our traditional Nativity plays provide a sentimentalised view of last-minute panic, with a mother about to give birth being turned away from inns that were full. But Kenneth Bailey (*Jesus Through Middle Eastern Eyes,* SPCK, 2008) identifies a number of things that we have misunderstood from the account in Luke 2. Joseph was returning to his village of origin, and as soon as he got there and told them whose son he was, he would have been welcomed. Joseph was of royal descent, from the family of King David, a family famous in Bethlehem. How could Joseph show up there and not be welcomed? Furthermore, in most cultures a woman in childbirth receives special attention. There would have been women there who were going to pay attention and it would be an unspeakable shame on the entire village for Mary to be ignored and left. Also, Mary had relatives in a nearby village: in the months before the birth of Jesus she visited her cousin Elizabeth. So if Joseph had failed to find shelter in Bethlehem he would have turned to those family members just a few miles away.

So where does the over-sentimentalised story – the idea of no room in the inn – come from? When the Samaritan was taken to an inn it's a completely different word: it was a travellers' inn, a place where you could hire a room. The inn in the story in the birth of Jesus is a translation of the word for house and in those simple houses there would be an animal area and mangers where they could get food during the night when they were kept inside to keep the house warm. That would be at one end of the house and in a slightly better-off house there would be a guest room on the other end. And the Bible is saying that the family they were staying with already had guests, so the guest room was already full and they had to be with the family in the one room and the baby was born there. As with all poorer people, babies were wrapped in cloths. And the manger *was* there, filled with straw and he would simply be laid there. So, it was a poor home where Christ was welcomed.

For all sorts of reasons, Christmas has been over-sentimentalised and not only is it now a *secular story* it's also commercialised – it's just shopping, materialism, a mad, mad pursuit. But for us there is a *sacred story*.

In Matthew 1, it says that Jesus was conceived by the Holy Spirit. He came as a fulfilment of the words of the prophet who said that he would bring God to be with us, Emmanuel. When the Magi came they asked for the one born King of the Jews. They went to a palace but they found him in another place. Herod asks, 'Where will Christ then be born?' and the wise men among them said, 'The prophets say he will be born in Bethlehem.' The Magi went to Bethlehem and there they met him and worshipped him.

These Gentile wise men came after the shepherds and worshipped Jesus. The shepherds were seen as unclean people: they were Jews but they were unclean Jews. So unclean Jews come and worship him and then wise Gentiles come and worship him and here, where Jesus begins his life, is his power bringing reconciliation between

Jew and Gentile; no other power on earth will ultimately bring the peoples of this world together but Christ. He is the unifier of the unclean and the wise, the Jew and the Gentile.

In the Bible there are little pictures of the unbelievable wonder, power, beauty and otherness of who this baby born into a manger truly is. He will have David's throne and he will reign for ever (Luke 1:32–33). And when Elizabeth saw the pregnant Mary coming to her she understood something. 'Why am I so favoured, that the mother of my Lord should come to me?' (Luke 1:43). And later we read about Simeon, who says, 'My eyes have seen your salvation' (Luke 2:30). Have you had your eyes open to see what this season is all about? Don't be deceived by the manger and the simplicity of a peasant's home, but understand who Jesus truly is.

It doesn't matter how many services you go to, how many carols you sing, how many people you spend time with – until you have a revelation you will not understand what this story is all about. You need a revelation. What sets us apart as Christian people is that God in his love and mercy has brought a revelatory understanding to us of what the story of Christmas and the gospel message is all about. That we were lost people and that God sent his Son into the world to save us. And once we have that revelation, once we know what the story is truly about, then we have to respond. There is an action required of us.

- As soon as Joseph understood what was going on, he took Mary and loved and cared for her until the time came. There was an action on his part.

- What happened to Mary was out of this world. But she believed, she responded and she spoke out words of acceptance.

- Elizabeth expressed her faith.

- The shepherds were urgent in their action. They hurried. There was an action, there was an urgency, there was a commitment.

- The moment they had understanding the wise men came from the east. They came and they worshipped.

If you understand the message you have to *do something*. What do you need to do? What do you need to say? Do you need to ask something? Do you need to believe? And who of us doesn't need to give in a new way? This is the action I believe that comes from response to a revelation of knowing the season.

Revd Canon David Shearman has been the Senior Minister of the Christian Centre, Nottingham, since 1977. It is a vibrant, growing church of over 1,400 people representing more than forty nationalities (see www.christiancentre.org). He also maintains a schedule of extensive preaching and teaching worldwide and is an Ecumenical Canon of Southwell Minster. He is married to Dorothy and has two grown-up children and four grandchildren. Someone once described David as 'a Pentecostal monk, with tears'.

GAFFA TAPE GOSPEL
Will Van Der Hart

Duct tape was originally developed during World War II for sealing ammunition cases. It was also used to repair military equipment, including jeeps, firearms and aircraft. The Army classify two types – 50 miles per hour and 100 miles per hour – depending on the speed at which you have to drive your vehicle for it to peel off! A more specialised product, known as gaffa tape, is preferred for many jobs because it does not leave a sticky residue when removed. In Finland, gaffa tape is actually called 'Jesus Tape', because it repairs everything!

In the past I have preached some comforting if not comfortable Christmas sermons, but I have started thinking about how difficult the past year has been for many people and how nice it is to retreat from the ensuing storm into the Christmas Nativity. Rather than being relevant to the challenges of these storms, Christmas can become an escape from them. What is actually a really uncomfortable scene has been softened with glowing fairy lights and cotton-wool sheep.

God set up the Nativity scene for a purpose and he doesn't want us to edit out the bits that we don't like. He doesn't want us to make the desperately uncomfortable and unseemly birth of Jesus into a cosy, romantic tableau. As in everything that God does, the message is both explicit and implicit, both visual and auditory. It wasn't an accident that the King of kings was born in a stable and laid in an animals' feeding trough – it *was* the message: the King of kings had moved into our neighbourhood, born into our mess, experiencing our pain and our problems.

Gaffa tape has three core qualities: it repairs everything; it is impossibly strong; and when it touches you, you can't get it off.

I believe that the church is the hope for the healing of broken towns and hurting nations. The Word become flesh and moved into *our* neighbourhood. We should remember how Jesus identified with the oppressed and the homeless. In the Nativity God visually demonstrates that restoration and repair has literally come into the centre of our real and troubled lives.

Jesus had come to touch the lives of young mothers like Mary, single mothers, struggling mothers, first-time fathers like Joseph, adoptive fathers, stepfathers, and parents in financial difficulty who may be facing homelessness or crippling mortgage repayments.

The King of kings had come not to rub shoulders with royalty but 'to seek and to save the lost' (Luke 19:10), to align himself with shepherds, the outsiders of first-century society. The ultra-poor would be visited by angels, and the first to meet the Saviour of the world. He had come to repair and restore what was broken.

That is not to say that Jesus' message was just for the poor, but it was showing that God's priorities weren't the priorities of society at large. He had come to show the impossible strength of the gospel to those who had no strength of their own. As the Psalmist says, 'The LORD is my strength and my shield; my heart trusts in him, and he helps me' (Psalm 28:7). And once touched by the message the shepherds couldn't shake it off; they were compelled to visit the manger stall and respond to God in worship. 'They hurried off and found Mary and Joseph' (Luke 2:16).

The Nativity is a picture of a God who came to all peoples, all cultures, all ethnicities. The second group of people to visit the Son of God were three Middle Eastern, probably Persian, astronomers. God had come for the materially wealthy too, for the highly educated and scientific – for the City bankers and top professionals. (But he has also come into the lives of illegal immigrants, European migrant workers, political exiles and trafficked and exploited peoples.)

Not only were the Magi invited by God, via the star, they were fully complicit in the restorative work that God has come to do. They brought gold for the King of kings and olibanum (frankincense) which is derived from the Arabic *al-lub* ('the milk'), a reference to it being a milky sap. Frankincense has long been used for its medicinal and soothing properties and in the ancient world was used for treating depression. God had come for the mentally and emotionally broken too. Jesus was to be our priest and our healer. Myrrh was an embalming ointment (John 19:39) that signified the greatest repair: Jesus was born to die for the sins of the world, in order that the relationship between God and us might be stuck back together again.

The Jews had always felt that God's revelations were for them alone, but here God was inviting their cultural enemies to the very moment when he entered the world. He came 'first to the Jew [the shepherds], then to the Gentile [the Magi]' (Romans 1:16). This 'Gaffa Tape Gospel' repairs the relationship that has been broken between humanity and God, and between people.

The Gaffa Tape Gospel has restoration at its very heart; it speaks directly into our prejudices, our divisions. It is the gospel for immigration, integration and collaboration. It takes away our petty differences and offers us true unity in head and heart, unity under the headship and lordship of this tiny baby. As Paul says, 'He is before all things, and in him all things hold together' (Colossians 1:17).

This Gaffa Tape Gospel is for a hurting and dirty world, not for a sweet and sanitised one. But it is also for a broken you and a broken me. I believe in this repair, because I have experienced it. I was compelled to faith in Jesus, not by theology, or ecclesiology but by 'Gaffology'. My life was full of gaffes, mistakes and sins – my own and others'. My heart was broken and it needed to be stuck together again. But the tape on offer was never sticky enough; in fact, it did more harm than good. Then I heard that there was a repair for all my gaffes, once and for all: that 'Jesus Tape' was all I needed.

We are his church, reflecting and enacting the work that he did in our hearts and in our world. I know that the future holds many challenges, but I believe that this gospel, as the angel said, is 'good news that will cause great joy for all the people' (Luke 2:10). I would love to see even more people repaired, strengthened and compelled by it and I invite you to join me on the journey. 'Let us not become weary in doing good, for at the proper time we will reap a harvest if we do not give up. Therefore, as we have opportunity, let us do good to all people' (Galatians 6:9–10).

Revd Will Van Der Hart is Vicar of St Peter's, West Harrow, a vibrant and diverse suburban parish in North West London (www.stpetersharrow.co.uk). He is also an author and speaker with a special interest in emotional and mental health ministry. Will is married to Louie, a Christian journalist, and they have two children. For more details, see www.mindandsoul.info (twitter.com/@vicarwill).

GATHERED TO THE LIGHT
Justin Welby

We are living in an age of scattering and separation, where we deal less and less with each other, and then find ourselves ill-equipped to face crises that require solidarity and sacrifice. Not so much at an individual level, where there is still much selflessness, where the weak are loved and cared for, and where communities exist and flourish. But at a political level, and in the drive to ever higher returns in much of the world of financial services, an institutional distance has grown up between what people do and the consequences of their actions. It means we look first to ourselves and push our own interests, and the richer we become the more that seems to happen.

Technology makes it easier for us to be scattered and still in touch, but without having to cope with each other. Technology hides the impact of actions. It may be the pilot of a drone in Afghanistan, living in Arizona, fighting a war by remote control between dropping his kids at school and picking them up; or it could be a cocoa trader at an investment bank altering the lives of whole populations as he buys or sells. It may be useful and beneficial, or impersonal and selfish. Either way, there is more distance than in the past. Our ethics, our morals and our lives have been increasingly touched by scattering and separation. And so when we do rub into each other, we find it harder, we grumble more.

Christmas stands against scattering and separation. It is a time of gathering. We gather with friends, with church, with family. We are especially conscious of those spending Christmas on their own. Food gathers us also – usually too much food!

Above all, the stories of Christmas are full of people being gathered and all of them were gathered to Jesus. They vary hugely as to who they were, and who they were was uncomfortable for the readers of Luke's Gospel. Shepherds in the fields, whether washing their socks by night (as an uncle used to sing loudly and determinedly every year) or not, were really not a good thing. They tended to be unreliable when tending other people's sheep and unpleasant when tending their own. As today, they were at the sharp end of the conflict between pastoralists and cultivators. They felt it was their eternal right to graze where they chose and never mind the crops. And, because they were often dealing with wild animals, they had weapons and knew how to use them. And Magi from the east were scarcely more welcome. They worried people, especially Herod. They were foreigners in a country where foreigners were bad news. But both these extremes were gathered to Jesus. Those who are gathered are surprising: from a religious leader's point of view the wrong ones for God, yet he gathers them.

And Jesus did not only gather the good ones who feature in crib scenes and Christmas carols. He gathered opposition and hatred from the first moments. Herod wanted to know what was going on, and sent soldiers to kill. They were gathered for evil. Jesus gathers people around him, some to follow him, others to kill him. And what they saw when they came together was both surprising and predictable. A baby, albeit in a manger. Odd, yes, but not that wrong. Babies do well in all sorts of places. This was a baby of a very poor family, in the meanest conditions. Predictable yet astonishing. The baby is God, and is worshipped. They have gathered to see all humanity wrapped up in the love of God, and seen in a baby. That is astonishing beyond words. It is unlikely, even absurd. This is not a predictable God, but God making himself vulnerable so that he is alongside us, so we can reach him and know him.

Jesus still gathers people, both for him and against him. The role of the church is to be like the angels, like the star, a signpost to who it is we worship. And that means that we, as Christians, must be both predictable and surprising. We come from a culture of scattering and separation, and we are pulled together by Jesus, to learn to be a community that is against the whole cultural tide of separation and scattering.

I was recently sent a cross of nails from a church which I helped reopen in 2002, in Baghdad. Then there were 170 people, today there are 2,500, with clinics and schools and food programmes. Why the nail? Because more than 300 people have been killed in those years. They have been transformed – they have gathered members of all denominations, from modern Pentecostal to the ancient churches of the East – and together they have served Christ. They have been passionate and effective, and have suffered for it. Authentic churches gather, and because they are gatherers across every barrier of class and race and history, they bring opposition, even hatred. So it was for the baby Jesus, so it is for us.

As with that church in Baghdad we face a choice today – as individuals, as a church, as a society – between light and darkness. Scattering and separation mean darkness; allowing ourselves to be gathered into the light of Jesus means light.

We have gathered to the light. We find that the light comes from a child, from a peasant in Galilee, from a man on a cross, from an empty tomb. It is an absurd litany of weakness, yet it is the light of the world. Let us allow the power of that light to enter us. Invite him into every aspect of life, find the transforming power of his light and life, so that we have faces to love, we are gathered to one another, we renew our hopes and receive the life and future and purpose that is God's call and plan.

The Rt Revd Justin Welby became the Bishop of Durham in September 2011. Justin studied Law and History at Cambridge University and then spent eleven years in the oil industry. From 1989 to 1992, Justin studied Theology at St John's College, Durham, and then spent three years as a Curate in Nuneaton, followed by seven as Rector of Southam, both in the Diocese of Coventry. In November 2002, Justin became a Canon of Coventry Cathedral. In this capacity, with Canon Andrew White and later by himself, he was responsible for leading Coventry's international ministry of reconciliation. From December 2007 Justin was Dean of Liverpool, responsible for the Anglican cathedral whose mission statement is 'a safe place to do risky things in Christ's service'. He has published a number of articles in English and French on issues of international finance, ethics and management and also on reconciliation. Justin is married to Caroline. They have five children.

THE WONDER OF CHRISTMAS PRESENCE
Paul Williams

For some people, Christmas will be marked by the arrival of a new member of the family – a new child, grandchild, son-in-law or girlfriend. And no matter how many well-worn traditions are observed on Christmas Day the actual presence of that *new* person will define the experience of Christmas for you.

For others, it's the *absence* of someone that will largely define Christmas this year. That may be someone now living abroad or visiting other relatives. More painfully it could be someone dearly loved who died this year – and no matter how smoothly things go and how many other people show up, the absence of that one person will define the experience of Christmas for you.

Then again, you may be preparing to spend Christmas with a familiar line-up of family and friends. But extract even one member from that familiar grouping and your experience of Christmas would substantially change. It is presence – the presence of someone – that defines not just our experience of Christmas but our whole experience of life.

Imagine how it would change the way you felt about Christmas Day if, at just before 3 o'clock in the afternoon, there was a knock on your door. As you glance out of the window you notice a line of very impressive-looking cars outside your house. You answer the door expecting to be asked for directions, but on your doorstep you find a tall, smartly dressed man. He tells you that Her Majesty the Queen wishes to deliver her Christmas speech to you personally this year.

A few moments later, the Queen is shown into your living room and, sitting in your best armchair, she delivers her message to you and your family. A lone trumpeter then strikes up the national anthem, and after you have dutifully sung to her, she bids you be seated, and stays for a slice of Christmas cake and a cup of tea. Twenty minutes later and you're waving her off from the doorstep as the cavalcade speeds down the road. Well, I wonder, would that encounter in any way change your experience of Christmas Day?

I guess it would. Still the same Queen's speech routine as every year – but this year the Queen herself is personally present to deliver it. She looks you in the eye as she speaks – the real presence of someone changes everything.

On that first Christmas night in a small town in the Middle East a presence entered our world in a way infinitely more striking and surprising than the visit of any monarch or superstar to your front door. God actually came among us as a human being – born as a tiny, fragile, adorable bundle of new life. But what difference can his presence really make to people like you and me?

First of all, *his presence can dispel unbelief.*

The writer Christopher Hitchens died recently. In 2007 he published a book called *God is Not Great*, (published by Twelve, an imprint of Warner Books, 2007) which made him a celebrity in his adopted homeland of the United States. Hitchens maintained his devout atheism even after being diagnosed with cancer in 2010, telling one interviewer, 'No evidence or argument has yet been presented which would change my mind.' But then he added wistfully, 'But I like surprises!' For all his doubts and determined objections Christopher Hitchens was right to expect surprises – the Christian faith is a long series of great surprises, beginning in a small town a day's walk from Jerusalem. Bethlehem played host to the greatest surprise of all – God becoming a human being, born as a baby.

One of Hitchens often-quoted arguments against Christianity was that, 'Exceptional claims demand exceptional evidence.' I don't think John in his Gospel would argue with that for one moment. In his opening he writes this: 'The true light that gives light to everyone was coming into the world ... We have seen his glory, the glory of the one and only Son, who came from the Father, full of grace and truth' (John 1:9,14).

At the heart of the Christmas story is the belief that God came into our world in human form – and his purpose was not to make things harder by pointing out our faults but to set us free to enjoy life through his guiding presence. Whichever way you approach the big issues of life and faith I think this demands a closer look. It's clear the Gospel writers were convinced that God's presence can dispel unbelief, and they were not afraid to present the evidence – in fact, many of those first Christians staked their very lives on this evidence.

Secondly, **God's presence can overcome un-forgiveness.**

All across the world on Christmas Day family gatherings will take place in the shadow of un-forgiveness. Amid the clink of glasses and the choruses of 'Merry Christmas', there'll be people who long to be reconciled to someone they love. Giving and receiving forgiveness sounds so simple, but it's the greatest roadblock to peace in relationships, in families and among nations.

John's Gospel tells us that Jesus came 'from the Father, full of grace and truth'. Jesus wasn't afraid to say tough things to people – he exposed the truth about human relationships. But the one who is full of truth is also full of amazing grace.

Some of the biggest economies of the world are currently trying to manage their financial deficits, but there is another kind of deficit that has the potential to do far more damage to human flourishing and that's a deficit of grace. The writer John Ortberg points out in *Love Beyond Reason*, (published by Zondervan, 1998) 'We don't live in a very grace-filled world. In this world you get what you pay for. You reap what you sow … But living by grace and remembering grace, is what keeps love alive. And losing touch with grace is a love-killer.'

No one knows more about the condition of our hearts than the God who made us, and yet when we allow his presence into our lives, the first thing we receive is his forgiveness for all our sins. It's a free gift from God, but it's not cheap! Jesus defeated the power of sin and death for ever by giving his own life for us. The cross of Christ was the only way to transform a world in desperate need of God's forgiveness. And it's out of the experience of being forgiven that we find new strength to go on forgiving others.

Finally, **God's presence can also remove deep-down loneliness.**

You can spend your Christmas in the finest of homes, around a warm fire, with plenty of family and friends in attendance and yet still feel desperately alone. The most terrible aspect of deep-down loneliness is that it can never be cured by simply adding more people to the equation – or more success, more money or more anything – because real loneliness is that part of us that's searching for significance.

Well, the birth of the Christ-child, the presence of 'God with us', rings a bright bell of hope in a lonely world struggling for significance. John wrote, 'To all who did receive him, to those who believed in his name, he gave the right to become children of God ...' (John 1:12).

You may spend this Christmas surrounded by many, or just a few, you may approach this Christmas in prosperity or up to your neck in financial worries, but if Jesus is present in your life, then you're more significant than you could ever know – you have become a child of the living God. So no wonder we're meant to celebrate Christmas!

This is the real Christmas gift that God offers to the human race: his loving presence that dispels unbelief, overcomes un-forgiveness and removes loneliness.

The Rt Revd Paul Williams became Area Bishop of Kensington in March 2009, having spent the previous ten years as Rector of St James, Gerrards Cross with Fulmer in Buckinghamshire. Paul's specific ministry interests are in the areas of Leadership Development, Church Growth and Children's Ministry. Having trained for ordained ministry at Wycliffe Hall in Oxford, he served a curacy in the London Diocese at St James, Muswell Hill, and then as Associate Vicar at Christ Church, Clifton in Bristol. Prior to ordination he studied Theology in Durham and served as full-time Youth Minister at St Andrew's, North Oxford. Paul is married to Sarah and they have three sons. He is enthusiastic about all sport, a keen fell-walker, and enjoys messing around in a Canadian Canoe on the River Thames close to their home in Twickenham.

THE GOVERNMENT WILL BE ON HIS SHOULDERS

N.T. Wright

To us a child is born, to us a son is given, and the government will be on his shoulders. (Isaiah 9:6)

Unless you sigh with relief at those words, you haven't really been listening. What we need now, more obviously than ever, is someone to shoulder the burden, someone who can get under, pick up our multiple problems and carry them for us. And Christmas night, together with its senior cousin, the night of Easter, is the real night for which planet Earth was waiting and to which it must look back if it wants to know the way forward.

We place too much trust in our politicians because we place too little trust in God. And when our politicians let us down, all we can think of is how to find another politician, one who will get it right this time.

At this point someone may be thinking, 'I picked this up to read about the baby Jesus, not politics.' Well, all right, let's talk about the baby Jesus. Why was he born in Bethlehem? Luke tells us it was because the then global superpower wanted to raise taxes, so told everyone to sign up and pay up. That's how the Middle East worked then and, with minor adjustments, that's how it works today. This was Caesar's world and, unless you were fool enough to try to buck the system, you shrugged your shoulders and did what you were told.

Yes, says Luke, but watch what happens next. The child who is born is the true king from the house of David. All the ancient prophecies spoke of him as the king, not of one small country far away, but of the earth itself, the world claimed by Caesar and taxed by Caesar, the world where the rich get rich at the expense of the poor while telling them they are giving them freedom, justice and peace. The world of empires from that day to this.

Luke's story digs underneath this story of everyday empire and undermines it with the explosive news of a different empire and a different *kind of* emperor. Jesus isn't simply another politician who will let people down. His way of establishing God's justice and peace on the earth was different to the usual power games and money games. We are hungry for exactly that difference.

Think back to Isaiah 9:2–7 and listen to the hunger for hope. 'You have shattered the yoke that burdens them, the bar across their shoulders, the rod of their oppressor': good news for a people, like so many today, hopelessly enslaved by debt or force of arms or a combination of both. 'Every warrior's boot used in battle and every garment rolled in blood will be destined for burning, will be fuel for the fire': good news for a people, like so many today, who find themselves caught up in wars they neither started nor wanted. And we, who hear these sorrows, are implicated, since the debts of far distant people are incurred in the same way that our own credit card bills and overdrafts are incurred, by rich banks luring people in over their heads and then demanding interest upon interest; and the wars of people far away are often fought with weaponry manufactured in rich countries and paid for with the loans we have made and on which we continue to charge the victims compound interest.

And Isaiah cries out that it's time for a different kind of world, a different kind of empire. That's what the Christmas message is all about: the coming of the world's true king, the one who stops wars, forgives debts and establishes true justice and judgement in the earth. But how does he do this? How can we prevent the Christmas message being more than just a fantasy to help us forget the dark reality for a day or two?

The Gospels tell of this child growing up and starting to put God's Kingdom into operation wherever he goes. This is what it looks like when God is running things. The world gets turned the right way up. The Wonderful Counsellor goes to work, dealing with individuals but also confronting the systems which had enslaved them, and upsetting the slave-masters. The Mighty God strides through Galilee feeding the hungry, healing the sick, rescuing people and restoring creation itself. The Everlasting Father is seen mirrored in the incarnate Son, giving himself totally to his beloved world. Jesus, from his earliest beginnings with a price on his head, through to his riding the donkey into Jerusalem, shows what it looks like when the Prince of Peace is on the move. He comes to get God's Kingdom off the ground, taking upon himself the full force of the world's cruel systems – the political and economic enslavement from which we still suffer – so that the power of evil can be broken and something new may take its place. This is what the alternative looks like. Some mock it as irrelevant, but it is all too relevant, a rumour of hope that the powers of the world do their best to hush up.

We need to think of different ways of ordering our world. And the best way is the Jesus-way, the baby-in-the-manger way, putting the vulnerable and the poor first and working out from there, instead of hoping that if the very rich can only help out the very rich then the poor will somehow benefit eventually. We need new economic principles, and new social and political principles. Now is the time to be working on them and we who worship the Christ-child need to be ready to speak up into that debate. We need to speak up out of a context where we are already at work, doing the Kingdom on the street, in our families, schools and offices, in local and national government, education, business, administration and, yes, even in church.

'The government shall be upon his shoulders': that is the good news of the gospel. But Jesus always exercises his authority through the healing and renewal of human beings, calling them as he called his first followers to the difficult but glorious task of working as his agents. Hence the to-and-fro between worship and witness, between what happens at the altar and what happens down the street. With the story of the Christ-child in our hearts, and the Spirit of Jesus giving us energy and direction, we are called to be Kingdom-bringers in whatever sphere we can. We have to think globally and act locally, campaigning for big issues like debt remission and climate change, and working on local issues like housing, asylum and unemployment.

The Kingdom of the Christ-child gets to work when we stop, look in wonder once more at the baby lying in the manger and, like Mary, ponder in our hearts what it all means. Only through deep devotion to the child who is born to us, the Son who is given to us, can we make sure that the government really *is* upon his shoulders. Let us celebrate the fact that the government is upon his shoulders, and go out into a new year to face the darkness with the news of a great light.

Prof. N.T. (Tom) Wright is a native of Northumberland. After graduating from Oxford University, he did a doctorate on the apostle Paul and was ordained, serving thereafter in a variety of academic and pastoral posts in Oxford, Cambridge and Montreal before becoming Dean of Lichfield, then Canon of Westminster and then Bishop of Durham (2003–2010). He is now Professor of New Testament at St Andrews. He has written over fifty books, both scholarly and popular, including the academic series 'Christian Origins and the Question of God' and the popular 'Everyone' commentaries on the New Testament, with the accompanying translation 'The New Testament for Everyone'. He is married to Maggie and they have four children and three grandchildren. Further details can be found at www.ntwrightpage.com.

CHRISTMAS SWORD
Philip Yancey

'Do not suppose that I have come to bring peace to the earth. I did not come to bring peace, but a sword,' Jesus told his disciples, twelve fresh recruits who on hearing this must have wondered what they were getting into. Jesus would later rebuke Peter for wielding a literal sword, and by that time all twelve must have had at least a hint of the broader scope of Jesus' words.

Jesus' 'sword', the instrument of a new Kingdom, brought division to family, neighbourhood and nation, and in general disrupted the tidy composition of planet Earth. As the Misfit in one of Flannery O'Connor's stories puts it, 'Jesus thrown everything off balance.'

This Christmas season, as I reread the familiar account in Luke 1 – 2, it struck me that the shadow of a sword hangs over Jesus' birth as well. We tend to recall the story in cheerful tones, having heard its words recited singsong style by children decked out in their parents' hemmed-up bathrobes, surrounded by friends waggling sheep tails and donkey ears. That first Christmas, however, menace filled the air.

'He will be a joy and delight to you,' an angel prophesied to Zechariah about his son John (Luke 1:14) – yes, and a worry and a grief too, as the boy grew up and reports filtered in of him eating bugs in the desert and incurring the wrath of Herod. As for John, he seemed to recognise his more famous cousin *in utero*: 'the baby in my womb leaped for joy,' Elizabeth told Mary when she learned of Mary's pregnancy (Luke 1:44). Flash forward thirty years, though, when John would send a haunting question from prison, 'Are you the one who is to come, or should we expect someone else?' (Luke 7:20). John would feel the sword at its sharpest.

I love the ironies embedded in Luke's Christmas story. While news of Elizabeth's pregnancy spread like gossip throughout the hill country of Judea, and her son John became a local hero for a time, poor Mary had to slip out of town to avoid the ugly accusations, and her son would be chased from the neighbourhood by a murderous crowd. 'A sword will pierce your own soul too,' the old man Simeon warned Mary (Luke 2:35), a statement she no doubt pondered during her boy's tumultuous time on earth.

The angel Gabriel, indignant over Zechariah's lack of faith, rendered him temporarily mute and thus unable to vocalise the best news he'd ever heard. Joseph and Mary, far from home and robbed of the traditional serenade by neighbours at the birth of a son, instead got a choir of angels in the sky. The baby himself began life on earth as he would end it, wrapped in binding cloths as if suggestive of the restraints he accepted in visiting this dark planet. God's Son – 'the bread of life' he would later call himself – spent his first night in a feeding trough slimy with animal saliva and un-chewed food.

A historian, Luke carefully dates the birth stories: 'In the time of Herod king of Judea there was a priest named Zechariah' (Luke 1:5). That simple conjunction foretells a plot line that will define much of human history: the uneasy relationship of church and state. Herod the Great sought to kill the baby Jesus. The monarch's son, another Herod, would later behead Zechariah's son John as a party trick and torment Jesus in a mocking trial. And after Jesus' death Romans would persecute his followers, as would Mongols, Huns, Turks, Vikings, Russians, Chinese, Albanians, Arabians, Sudanese and a host of others.

Zechariah prayed for 'salvation from our enemies', a timeworn Jewish prayer that assuredly never got the answer he yearned for. Like so many who encountered Jesus, he expected a different kind of Messiah, one who would lead armies to triumph astride a stallion, not ride a donkey towards his crucifixion.

Of all the characters in Luke's birth story, Mary seems to have the best grasp of the sword about to descend. Though often set to beautiful music, her Magnificat has a fierce and revolutionary tone, with rulers scattered, with the proud and the rich sent away empty, even as the humble are exalted and the hungry filled. In a kind of counterpoint, Zechariah's song ends with a plea that sets a lofty tone for the spread of the good news about Jesus: 'The rising sun will come to us from heaven to shine on those living in darkness and in the shadow of death, to guide our feet into the path of peace' (Luke 1:78–79).

Looking back over two millennia of Christian history, I see much evidence of further disruption caused by Jesus' followers. At this very moment war sabres are rattling, the land of Jesus' birth convulses and bleeds, and the worldwide church shows more division than unity. I find myself repeating Zechariah's song of joy as an urgent prayer, wishing that the Messiah's visit would be seen as a dawning of light and annunciation of peace.

The angel choir announced Jesus' birth with the words, 'on earth peace, goodwill toward men' (Luke 2:14, *King James Version*). If only we men and women on the ground could live out those words that filled the sky that Christmas Day so long ago.

Philip Yancey describes himself as 'a pilgrim, recovering from a bad church upbringing, searching for a faith that makes its followers larger and not smaller'. He has written a number of award-winning books exploring central issues of the Christian faith, such as *The Jesus I Never Knew* (Zondervan, 2002), *What's So Amazing About Grace?* (Zondervan, 2000) and *Prayer: Does It Make Any Difference?* (Zondervan, 2006). Philip Yancey and his wife Janet, a social worker and hospice chaplain, live in the foothills of Colorado. For more information, see www.philipyancey.com.